# Cyanotype

## LEARN IN A WEEKEND

First published in the United Kingdom in 2025
by Skittledog, an imprint of Thames & Hudson Ltd,
181A High Holborn, London WC1V 7QX

*Cyanotype: Learn in a Weekend* © 2025
Thames & Hudson Ltd, London

Text © 2025 Victoria Glover

Photographer: Charles Emerson
Designer: Masumi Briozzo
Production: Felicity Awdry

Extra photography by Victoria Glover on
front cover and pages: 4, 24, 25, 30, 31, 34,
36, 38, 49, 50, 51, 52, 53 (upper section), 54,
55, 56, 57, 58, 59, 60, 61, 64, 65 and 66.

British Library Cataloguing-in-Publication Data
A catalogue record for this book is available from
the British Library

ISBN 978-1-837-76063-3

Impression 01

Printed and bound in China by C&C Offset Printing Co., Ltd.

MIX
Paper | Supporting
responsible forestry
FSC® C008047

Be the first to know about our new releases,
exclusive content and author events by visiting
skittledog.com
thamesandhudson.com
thamesandhudsonusa.com
thamesandhudson.com.au

# Cyanotype
## LEARN IN A WEEKEND

VICTORIA GLOVER

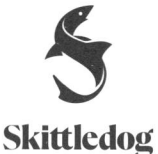

**Skittledog**

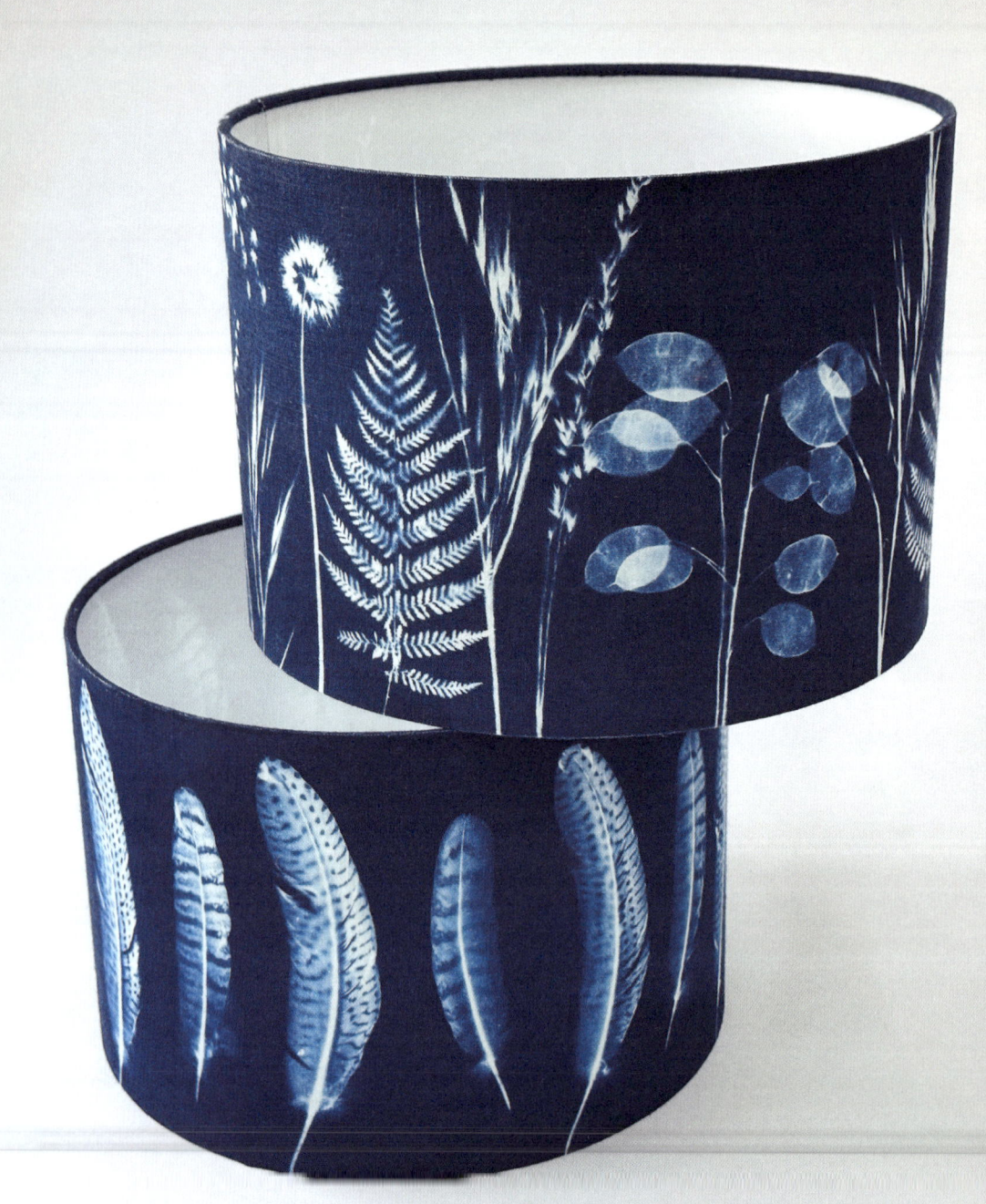

# Contents

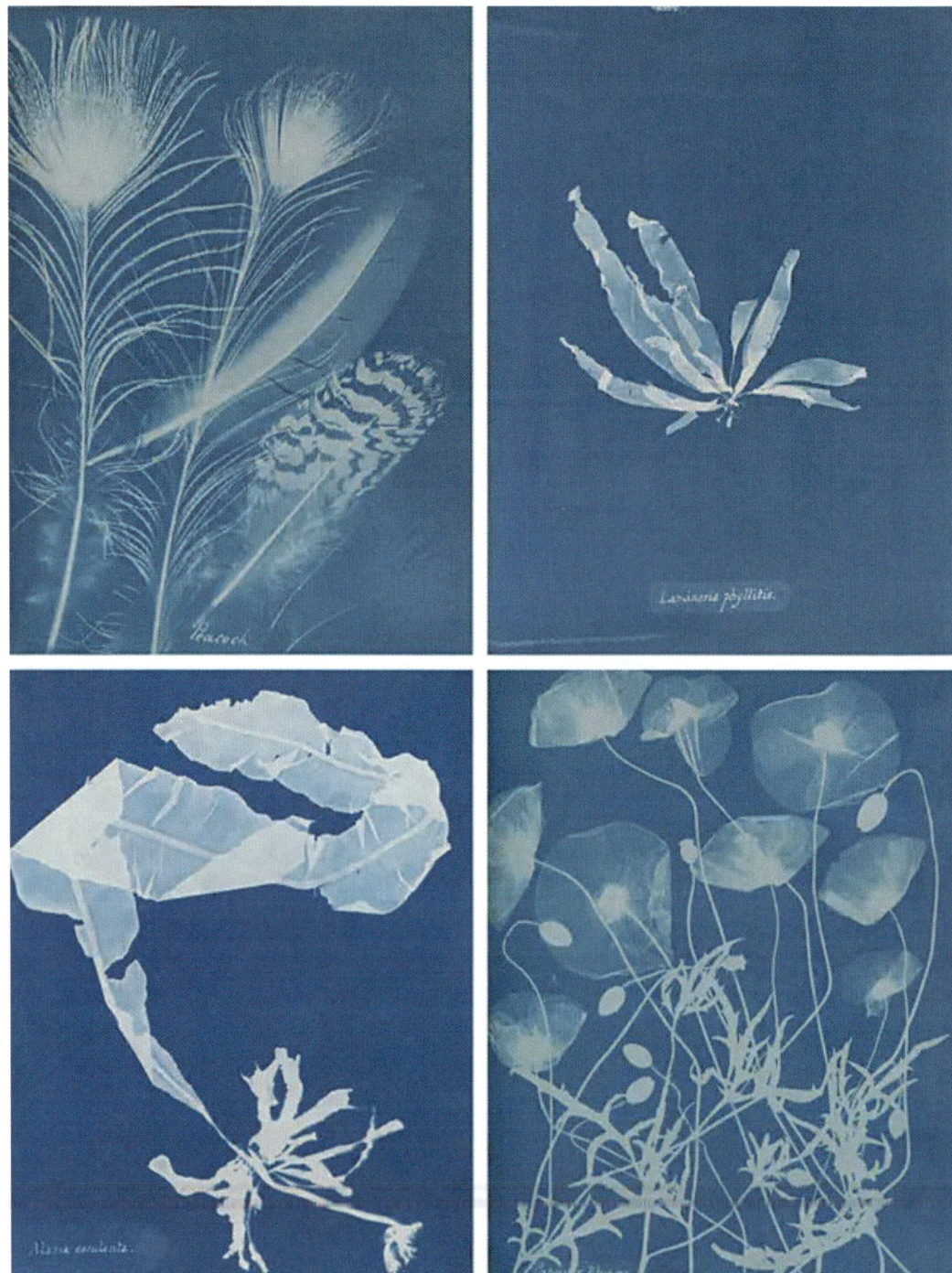

# Introduction

**Cyanotype prints bring together art and science in a fun – and surprisingly easy – process. With very little kit and just a bit of know-how, you can create one-of-a-kind prints and textiles using the power of the sun. Watch your designs develop in front of your eyes and they will breathe new life into old fabrics and fill your walls with unique artworks.**

Cyanotypes are simple photograms made by painting a chemical solution on to the surface of paper, fabric or wood to create a light-sensitive print. The images are created by placing the print in sunlight (or under a UV lamp) and made permanent by rinsing in water. Absolutely anything can be placed onto the coated surface to block the light, creating a fixed shadow print. Much of the fun of cyanotypes comes from finding the perfect objects to use in your design. You will see the world with fresh eyes when you realize that we're surrounded by inspiration at every turn, with potential in everything from feathers and ferns to vintage lace and old buttons.

Although cyanotypes were invented in 1842, the technique has recently grown in popularity as cyanotype artworks have been shared more widely on social media. The easy availability of the necessary chemicals combined with a minimal set-up means you will soon be making your own blueprints and exploring how you can push the process in different directions. The simplicity of cyanotype makes it a fun and accessible art form for all ages and abilities.

## The first cyanotypes

Invented in 1842 by Sir John Herschel, the technique was developed as a way of reproducing technical drawings, which is why even to this day, they are known as blueprints. Sir John Herschel was an acquaintance of Anna Atkins, who is known for her pioneering use of cyanotypes for botanical studies. She published these as a book, releasing 20 handprinted illustrated copies of her studies of British algae in 1843. Atkins is now recognized as one of the first female photographers and her work is preserved in museums.

Opposite: From *Photographs of British Algae: Cyanotype Impressions*, 1843, by Anna Atkins.

# The cyanotype process

While the method is simple, it is worth understanding how each stage of the cyanotype process works before you start.

# Tools and materials

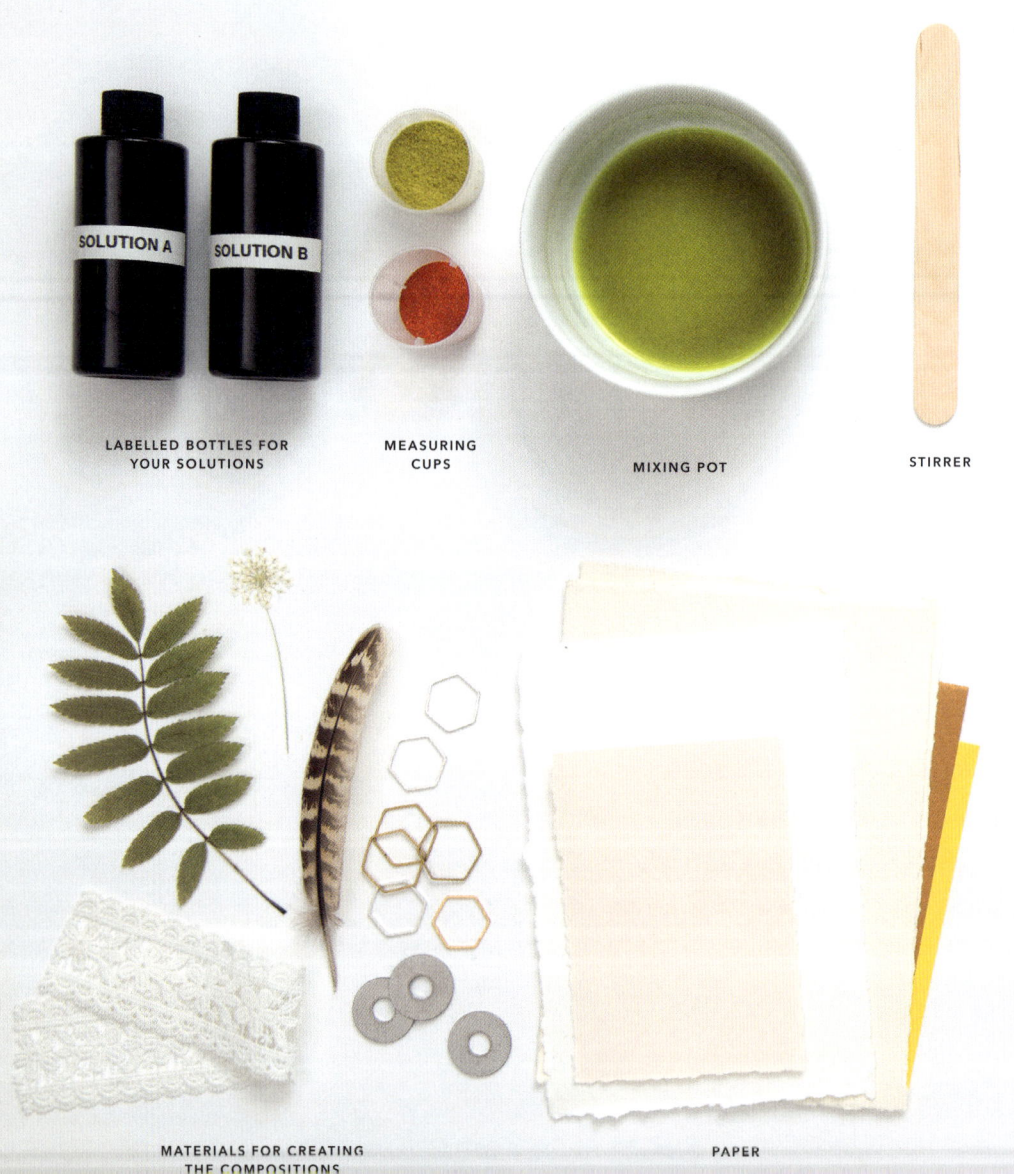

LABELLED BOTTLES FOR
YOUR SOLUTIONS

MEASURING
CUPS

MIXING POT

STIRRER

MATERIALS FOR CREATING
THE COMPOSITIONS

PAPER

PIECE OF MDF OR PLYWOOD BOARD AND
A SHEET OF PERSPEX OR GLASS

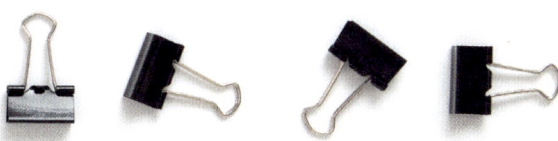

BULLDOG CLIPS

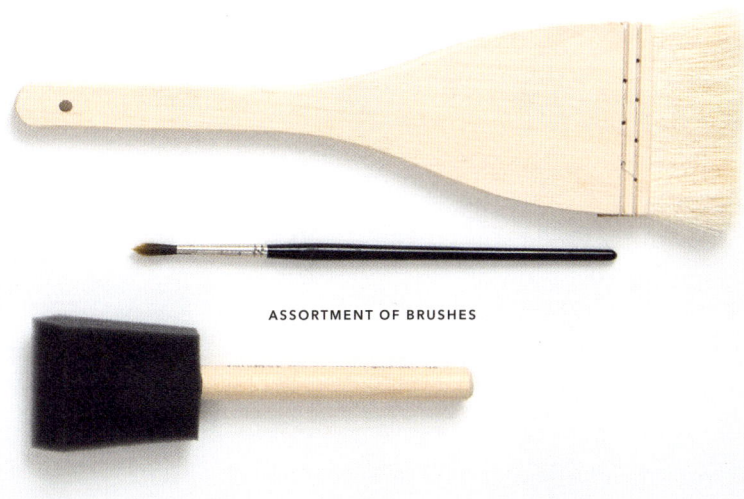

ASSORTMENT OF BRUSHES

# Coating the paper

Ready-prepared sun print paper is easily available and a great option, especially for making prints with children. However, it isn't difficult to prepare your own at home by following these instructions.

## Using cyanotype chemicals

To coat your own paper, fabric or other material, you will be working with potassium ferricyanide and ferric ammonium citrate. These chemicals aren't particularly toxic but you should take care not to get the liquid in your eyes and keep them out of reach of children to avoid accidental ingestion. Gloves are recommended, especially if you have sensitive skin. Wear an apron to protect your clothes from any splashes and protect your work surfaces with newspaper. The chemicals can stain the work surface, especially a wooden worktop if you don't wipe up any spills straight away. Generally, the cyanotype process is clean in comparison with other dyeing and printing techniques, but if you are concerned about working with chemicals, ready-prepared sun print paper produces great results (that's how I started nine years ago).

## The recipe

Pre-mixed chemicals are available from art and craft suppliers but if you are buying the chemicals in powder form, a reliable recipe for making up 200ml (6¾ fl oz) of cyanotype emulsion is:

### Solution A

10g (½oz) **potassium ferricyanide** mixed with

100ml (3½ fl oz) **distilled water**

### Solution B

25g (1oz) **ferric ammonium citrate** mixed with

100ml (3½ fl oz) **distilled water**

\* It's best to use distilled water as the minerals in tap water can affect the stability of the chemicals. After mixing, store in separate bottles until you are ready to use. It doesn't matter if the bottles are glass or plastic, but they should be opaque.

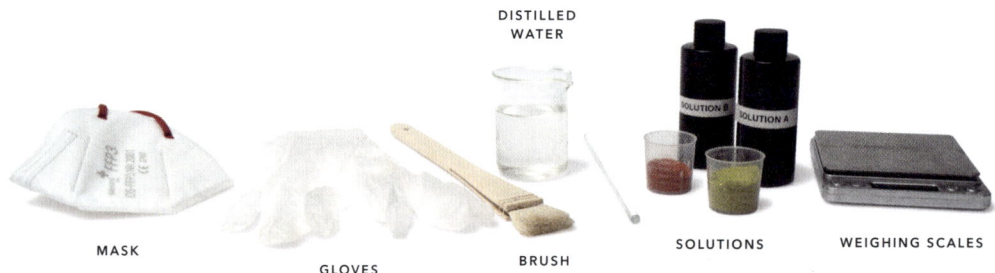

MASK

GLOVES

DISTILLED WATER

BRUSH

SOLUTIONS

WEIGHING SCALES

## Mixing the emulsion

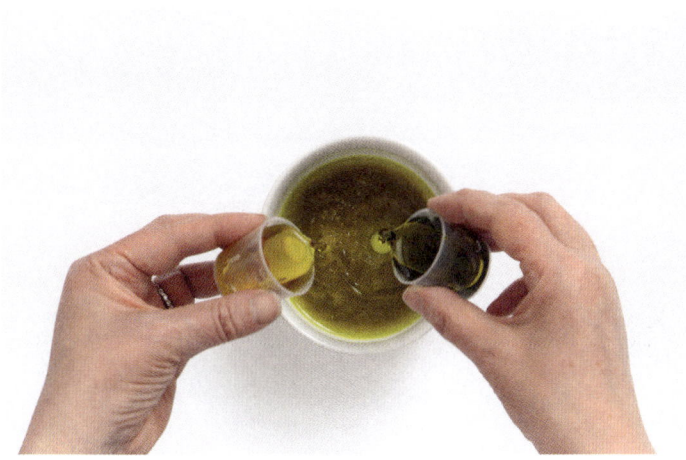

**1.** Follow the recipe shown opposite to make Solution A and Solution B. Using small measuring cups, mix equal parts of both solutions into another container. Don't make up more than needed as it will start to oxidize once you mix the two chemicals together. Aim to use the emulsion within a day or two, otherwise you will find that the whites in your print are less clean. Unused chemicals are safe to wash away down the sink in small quantities.

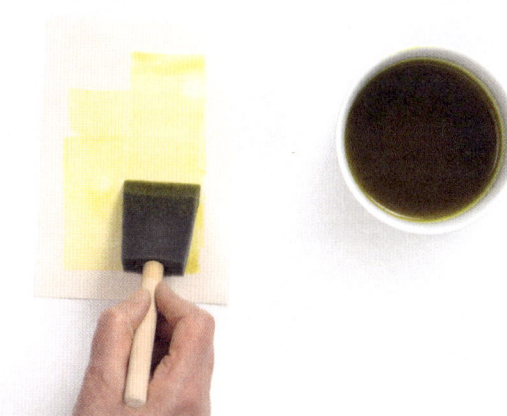

**2.** Once your emulsion is ready, apply it to the surface you are printing on with a brush. Aim for a thin and even coating on the print surface. If you apply too much, it will dry unevenly and be sticky to the touch and the resulting print will expose unevenly.

**3.** Once your paper is coated, it needs to be dried in a dark place to prevent exposing the print before you are ready. Good locations for this include a cupboard, a drawer or a box. Protect the drying area from your freshly coated materials if needed.

# Securing the materials

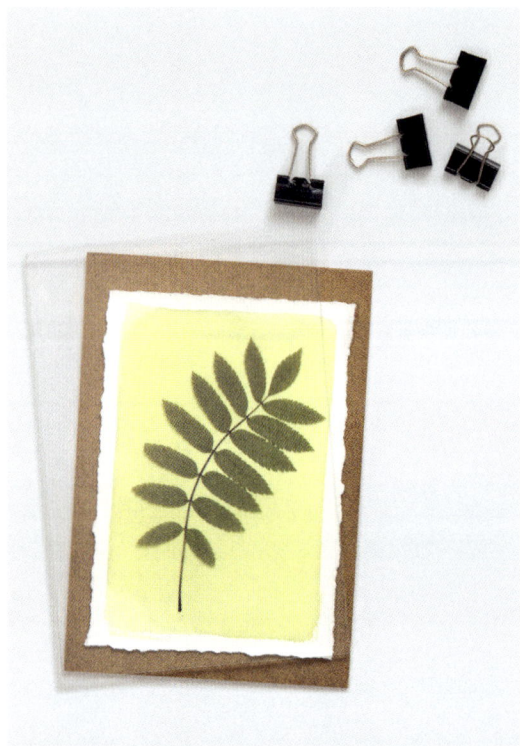

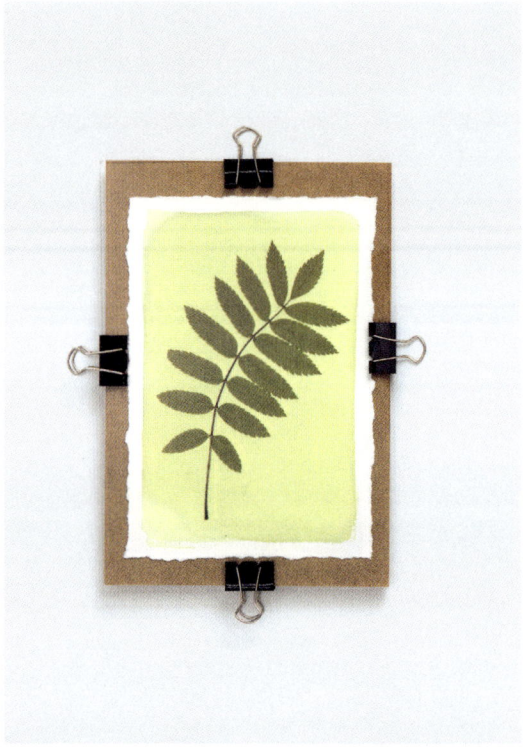

It's possible to use a photographic contact frame to secure your prints and subject matter, but a more accessible version is to use a sheet of Perspex or glass. Simply lay the sheet over your subject matter, pressing it down on your coated surface to achieve a clear result with crisp edges. If you are printing outside, the Perspex or glass is also very handy to stop the different elements moving or flying off in a breeze. If you are using a sheet of glass, protect yourself from the sharp edges by using gaffer tape around each side.

It is a good idea to steady your print materials and Perspex or glass sheet with a solid board (such as MDF or plywood) underneath. This is especially useful if you are arranging your subject matter inside and then carrying it outside to expose it. The Perspex or glass sheet should be the same size as the board and can be secured together using bulldog clips so that your subject matter is as flat as possible against the surface you are printing on.

# Exposing the print

The cyanotype process works by exposing a surface coated with the emulsion (see page 12), which is sensitive to UV light. This can come from either a UV lamp or by placing the print outside in the sun. Both methods work well – there is no difference in the end result. The chemicals in the emulsion react with the UV light and turn blue after being exposed and then rinsed in water. If you place your prepared print under a UV light or in the sunlight without placing anything on top to block the light, the whole surface will turn blue. If you place materials on top of your print, the UV light will be blocked in those areas and that part of your print will remain white (if your paper was white to start with).

The exposure time needed depends on a number of factors, such as the levels of UV when you place your print outside (affected by cloud cover and time of year). If you use a UV lamp to expose your print, the exposure will depend on how strong the UV light source is. The best way to find out in both situations is to start with a test print.

## Making a test print

To make a test print, use a strip of paper coated in emulsion. Block a section of the print with card and place it in the sun or under your lamp. Use regularly timed exposures: for example, move your card along your print at five-minute increments to gauge your ideal exposure. This is recommended at the beginning of every outside printing session to get an indication of how long you should expose your print to get your desired shade of blue. Bear in mind that UV levels are constantly changing depending on the level of cloud cover and the time of day – they are at their strongest between 11am and 4pm. If you're using a UV lamp, you will have a consistent light that you don't get when working outside, and you might not need to make a test print very often once you have worked out your optimum exposure time.

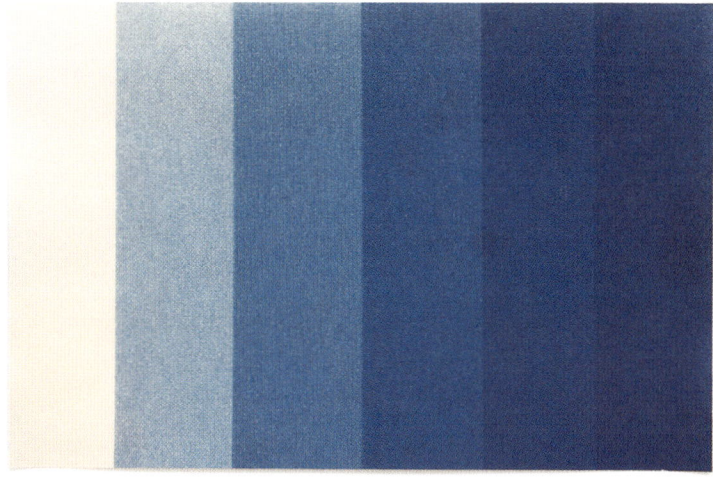

# Rinsing and drying

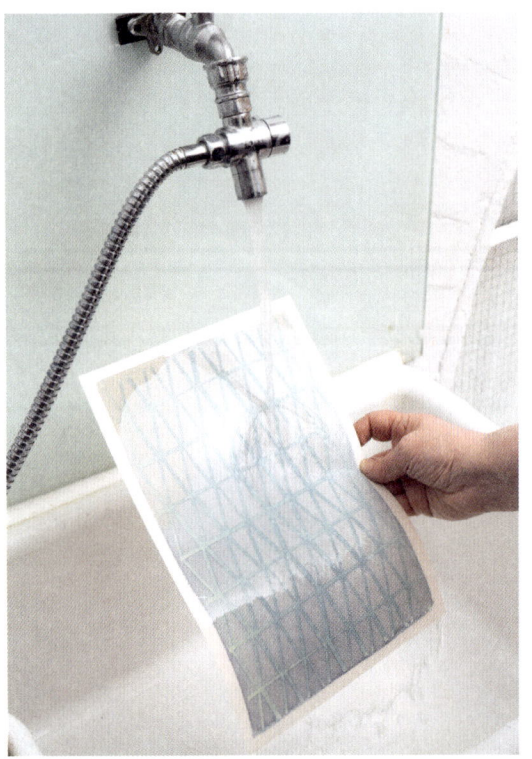 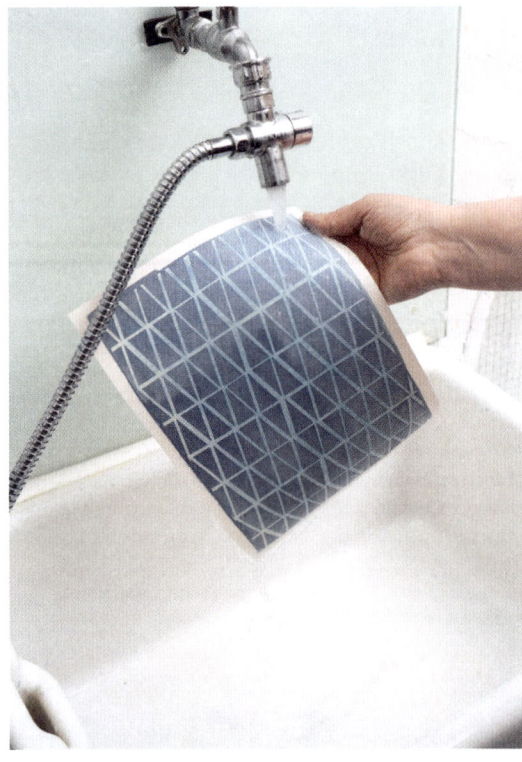

Once you've exposed your print, the next step is to bring it inside out of the sun or to remove it from under the UV lamp. Take away the object or objects and get ready to rinse the print in water. You can either place it in a tray with fresh water and agitate the tray, or rinse it directly under a tap until the water runs clear. The aim is to rinse away all the unexposed chemicals. As soon as you place the print in water, you'll notice that the emulsion starts to turn blue, apart from where you've blocked the light.

The more you rinse, the more the print will turn blue. Once you think you have rinsed away all of the unexposed emulsion, leaving clear white where your object was, your print will be ready to hang up to dry or to pat dry with paper towels. The print will gradually darken over the next 24 hours until it reaches its final shade of blue. After this, it won't darken any further.

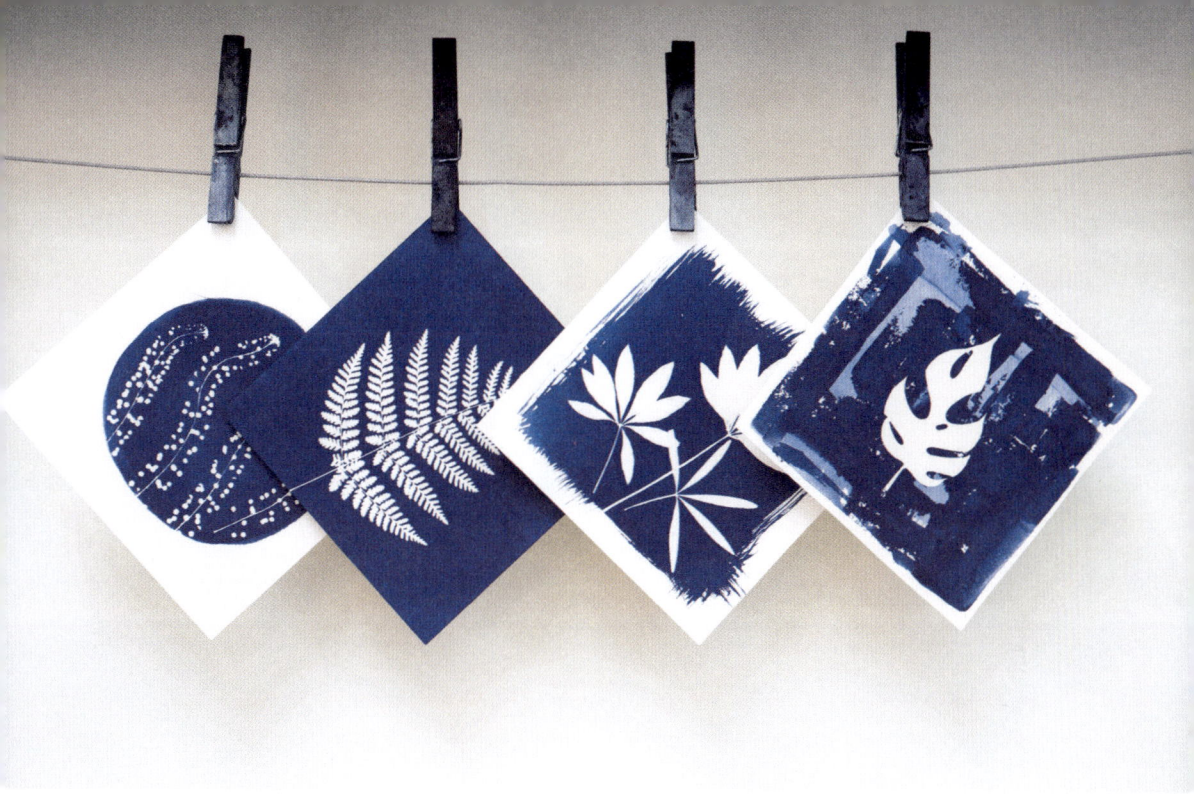

## Tips and troubleshooting

• During the rinsing stage, add a splash of hydrogen peroxide to your rinsing tray to speed up the development process. Without the hydrogen peroxide, the same dark blue will still naturally develop over 24 hours, but use this if you want to see your end results in an instant.

• Don't dry your prints outside as they can bleach slightly before fully developing.

• If your print is a faded blue or rinses away once you run it under water, your exposure time might not have been long enough. While it is exposing, look for a shade of brown or khaki developing: this is a good indication that end result will have a dark shade of blue.

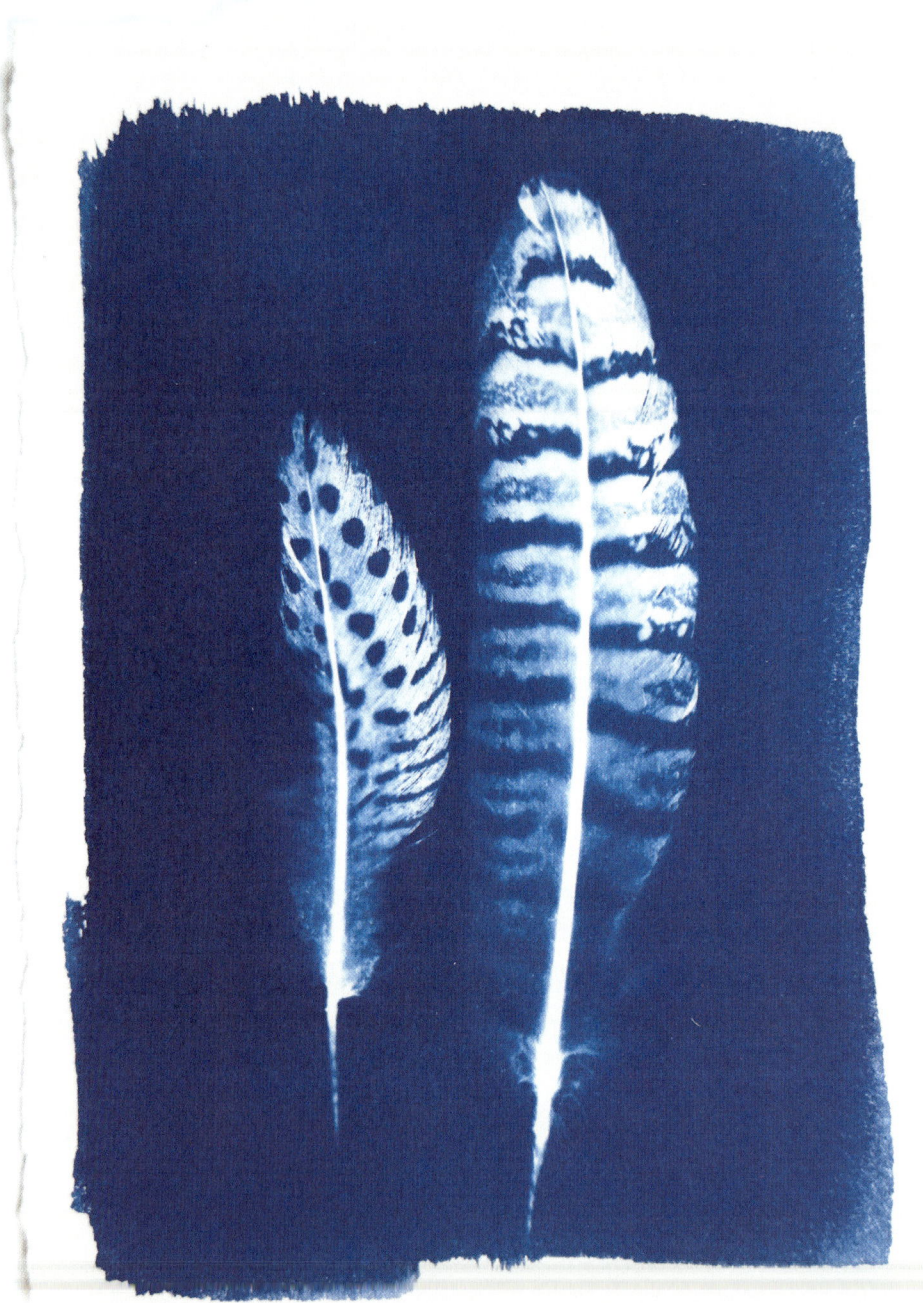

# Making your first cyanotype

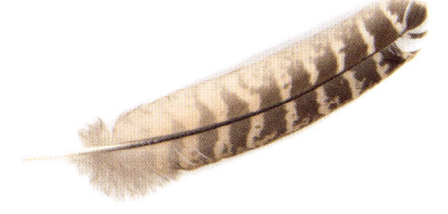

Now we have looked at the process in detail, these instructions show the steps to work through when making your first print. The first step only applies if you are coating the surface with the cyanotype emulsion yourself. If you are working with ready-prepared paper or fabric, skip to step 2.

**1.** Mix your cyanotype chemicals in a bowl following the instructions on pages 12–13. Lightly coat the surface of your paper with the emulsion using a brush – a foam brush will give you an even coating and a Japanese hake brush can give you textured, brushed-on edges. The trick is not to paint the solution on too heavily as it will dry unevenly and be sticky. You should be able to hold the print up and not have any of the solution run or drip off the surface.

**2.** When it is dry, place it on a board and arrange your objects onto the paper. You might find it easier to plan your composition in advance. Work inside and away from direct sunlight and, when you're happy with your design, place the Perspex or glass sheet fully over your print and secure with bulldog clips. If you're working with botanicals, the more contact you create between your subject and your coated surface, the more detail the resulting print will have.

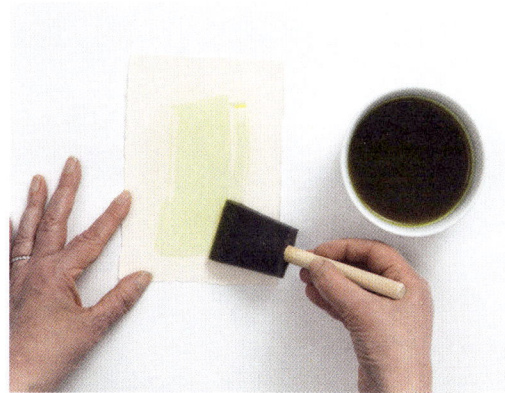

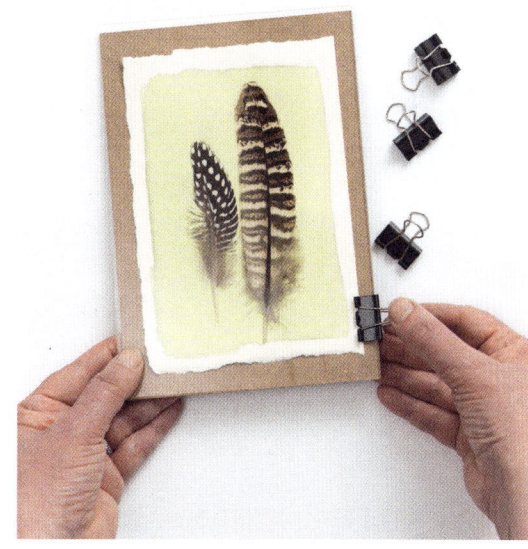

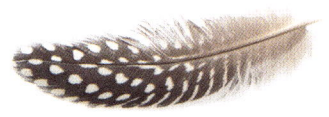

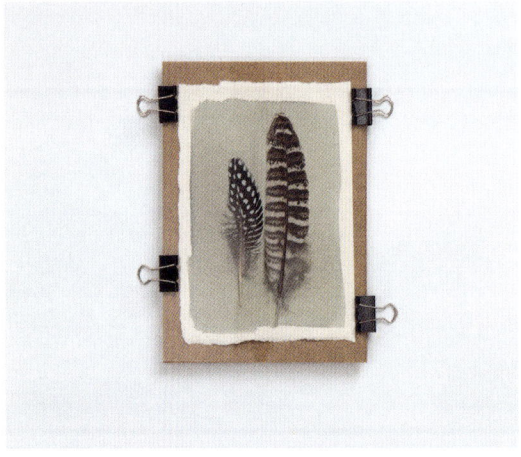

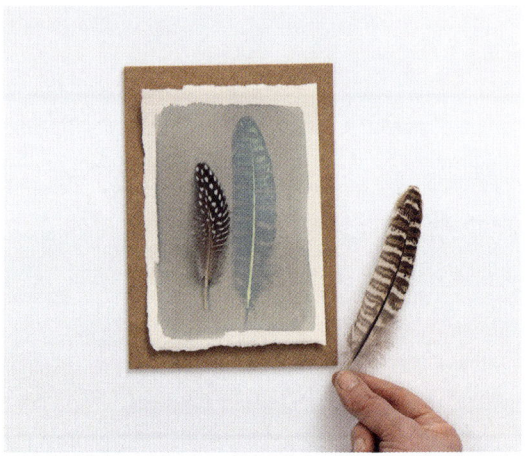

**3**. Start to expose your print, either outside in the sun or under a UV lamp. The amount of time you need to expose your print depends on many factors, especially if you're exposing outside, such as the time of year, the cloud cover and the time of day.

**4**. Bring the print back inside or take it out from under the UV lamp and remove your subject matter.

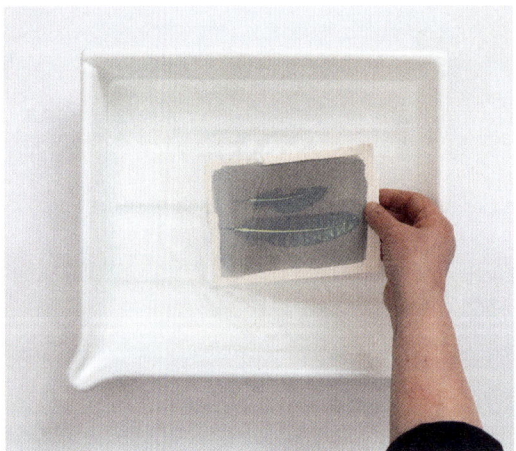

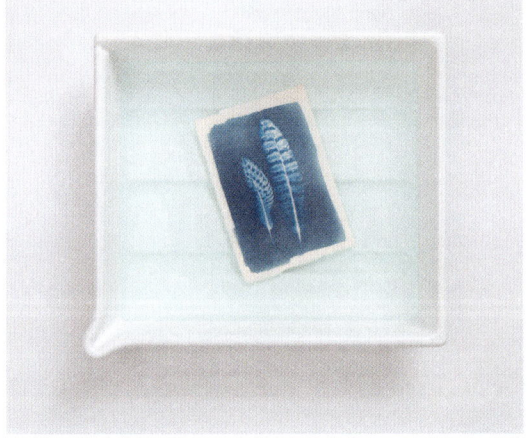

**5**. Rinse the print in a tray or under running water in a sink until the water runs clear.

**6**. Your print will gradually darken to its final shade of blue over the next 24 hours, but if you want to speed up the development process, rinse the print in a tray containing hydrogen peroxide (or use a spray bottle with diluted hydrogen peroxide) and then rinse under water again.

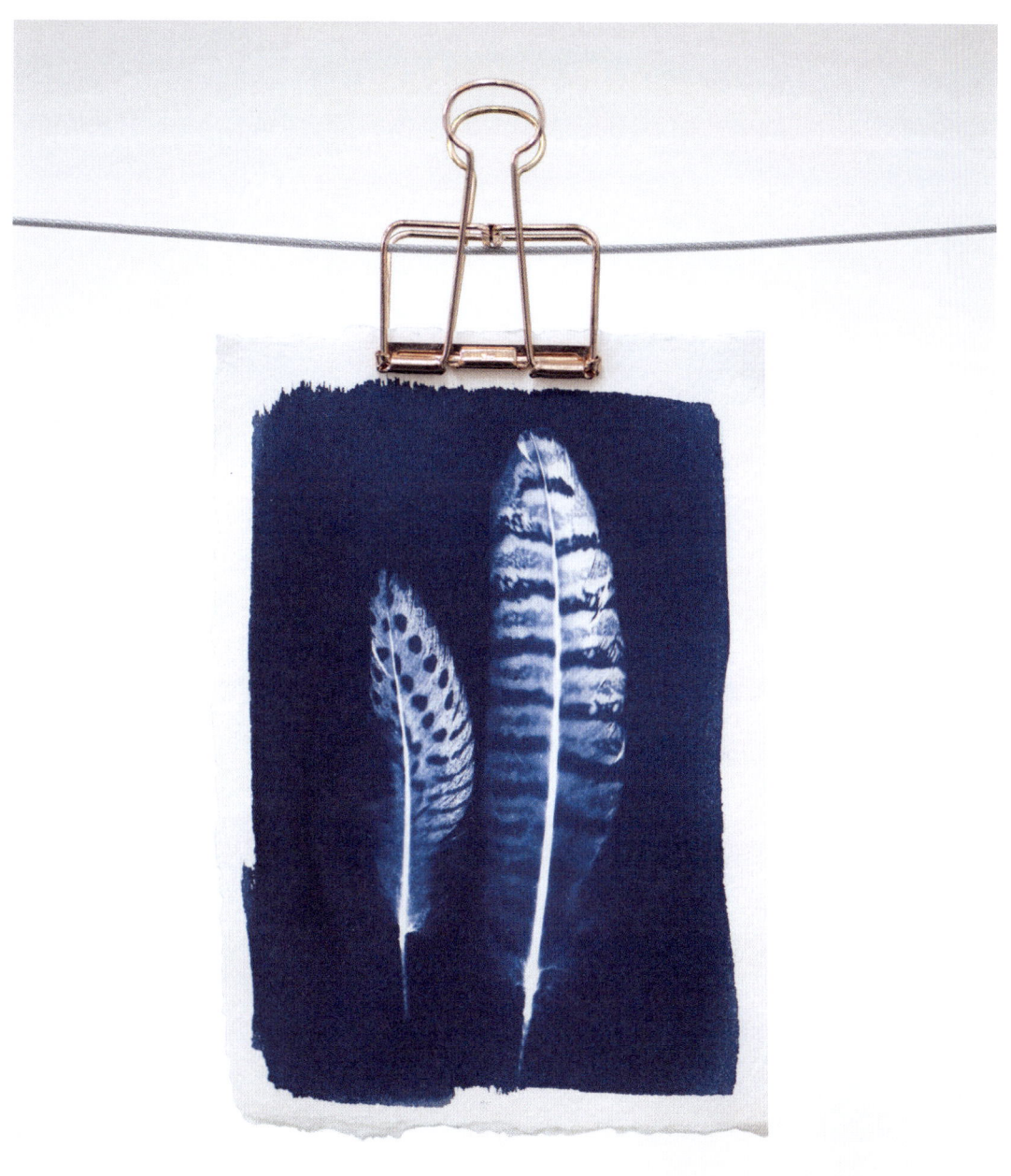

**7.** Peg up your print to dry or pat it with paper towels.
Your print will be stable after 24 hours.

# Creative choices

The creative part of cyanotype printing lies in the decision making and it helps to understand the potential outcomes of your choices before you begin the exposure.

# Choosing a surface

Traditionally, most cyanotypes have been printed on paper but there is much fun to be had from exploring other surfaces, such as fabric and wood. Treat them in the same way as you would your paper cyanotypes; there is no difference in the steps you need to take when coating, exposing and rinsing your substrate. Enjoy the added dimensions that these materials bring to your finished print.

## Wood

When printing on wood, look for interesting grain and always choose the lightest wood you can find for the best results. Birch plywood works beautifully for cyanotypes as it's light in colour and subtly grained so your resulting print shows up clearly.

## Different types of paper

The first thing to keep in mind when choosing paper is whether it will be sturdy enough to rinse in water. Cartridge paper is a good starting point while you familiarize yourself with making cyanotypes, but it can crease easily. Something sturdy, such as watercolour paper, print-making paper or mixed-media paper, is a good option. Each type of paper will react differently to the cyanotype chemicals, and part of the fascination of this process is finding the paper that gives you the best results – which can change depending on the result you are looking to achieve. There really is no definitive paper to use. Acid-free paper is recommended for the best and longest-lasting results.

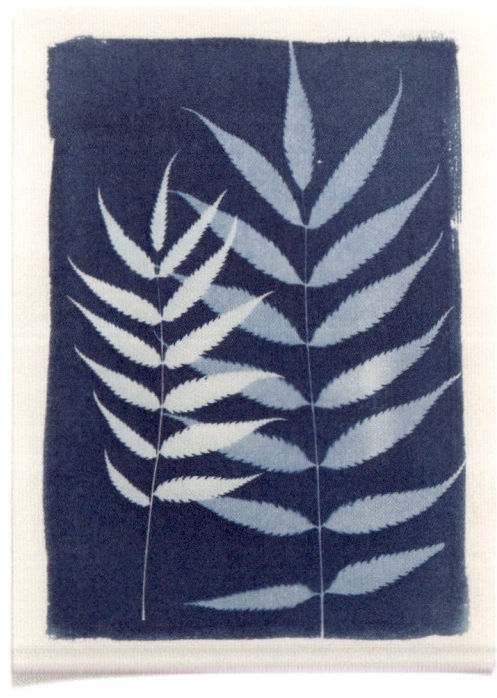

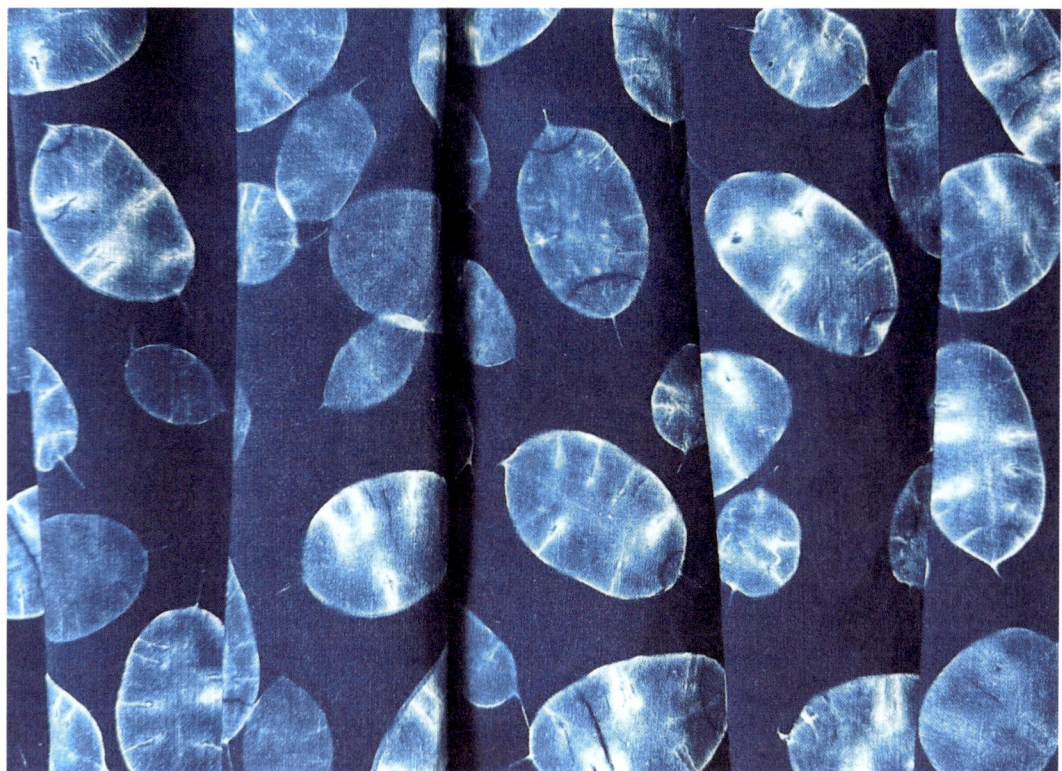

## Fabric

The cyanotype solution won't work on synthetic materials, so choose natural fabrics to get the best results. Cotton can give very crisp and photographic results, while linen results in a more textured print depending on the weave of the fabric. The best thing to do is to experiment and see what works and what doesn't.

There's something very satisfying about printing unique designs on fabrics, especially if you can then repurpose those fabrics into something else like a cushion, a lampshade or a wall hanging. You can even upcycle a faded pair of jeans, but remember that a cyanotype image is essentially a photographic image sitting on top of your fabric – it isn't permanently embedded into the fibres and it will fade with each wash. That's fine for something like a lampshade but not ideal for a T-shirt or scarf. If you do wash your printed fabrics, always use a low temperature and detergents that are free from phosphates and sodium carbonate, as you don't want to accidentally bleach your fabric. (If this does happen, see the toning with tannins section on page 44.)

The size of the fabric you are printing on is only limited by the size of the Perspex or glass you are using to flatten and secure your objects. If you want to print a large piece for a cushion or lampshade, bear in mind that you will need to source the same size Perspex or glass.

You can paint the cyanotype emulsion directly onto your fabric, which gives more control over the surface area you wish to cyanotype. Alternatively, you can place enough of the emulsion into a bowl and dip or soak your fabric into that. Note that fabric soaks up a lot more of the emulsion than paper does. You will need to hang the fabric up to dry in a dark place, so protect your floor and surfaces from drips.

# Printing on coloured paper

So far in this book we've only looked at working on white paper. Traditional cyanotypes are the classic Prussian blue and white prints – that's what makes them so recognizable – but you're not limited to blue and white. You can use any colour paper, as long as it's light enough to allow the cyanotype design to show through, and sturdy enough to rinse in water.

The cyanotype chemicals will always turn blue, but think about what happens if you use those chemicals on yellow or pink paper to create greens and purples. Have some fun trying out different types of coloured paper and card to see how the particular blue produced by the cyanotype chemicals shows up against those colours.

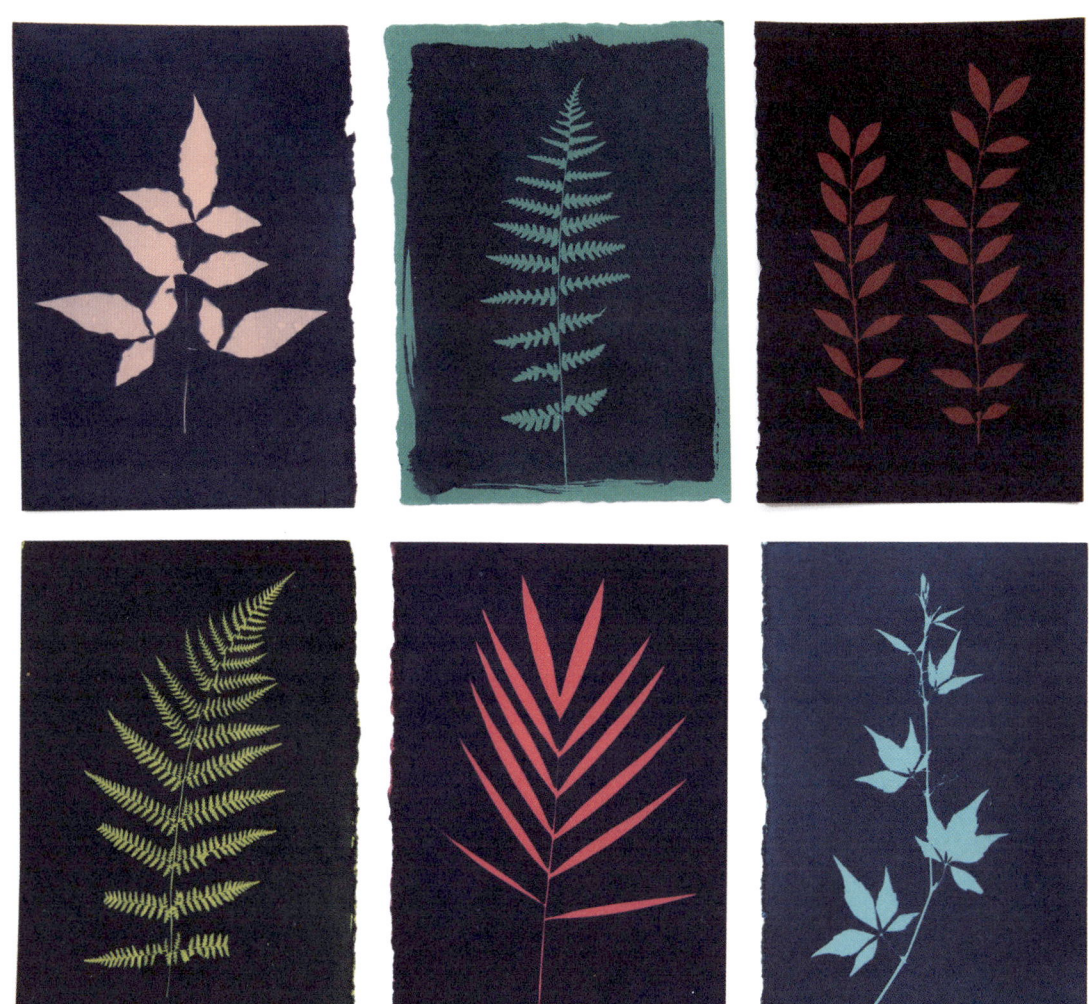

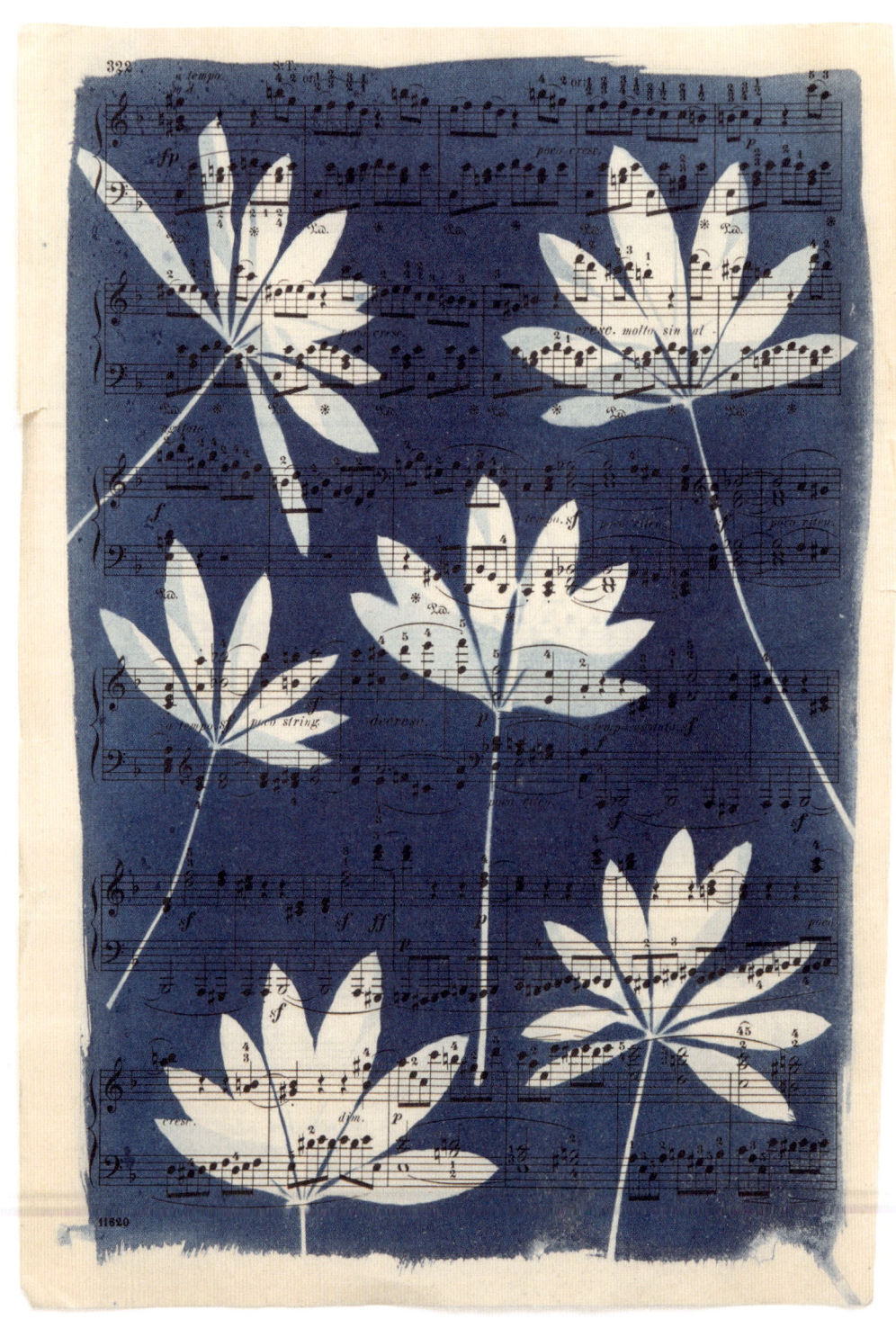

# Printing on vintage papers

Just as you can use different colours of paper, consider using vintage papers, such as pages from old books, sheet music or maps to add even more interesting qualities to your cyanotypes. These papers can make a wonderful background on which to coat your cyanotype solution, allowing the music notes or map designs, for example, to show through on your print where you block the light with your objects. The only thing you should take into consideration is that the print will need to be rinsed in water to fix it, so make sure that the paper you choose isn't too fragile.

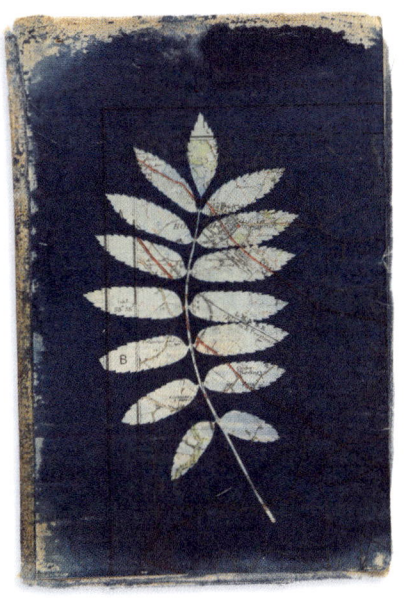

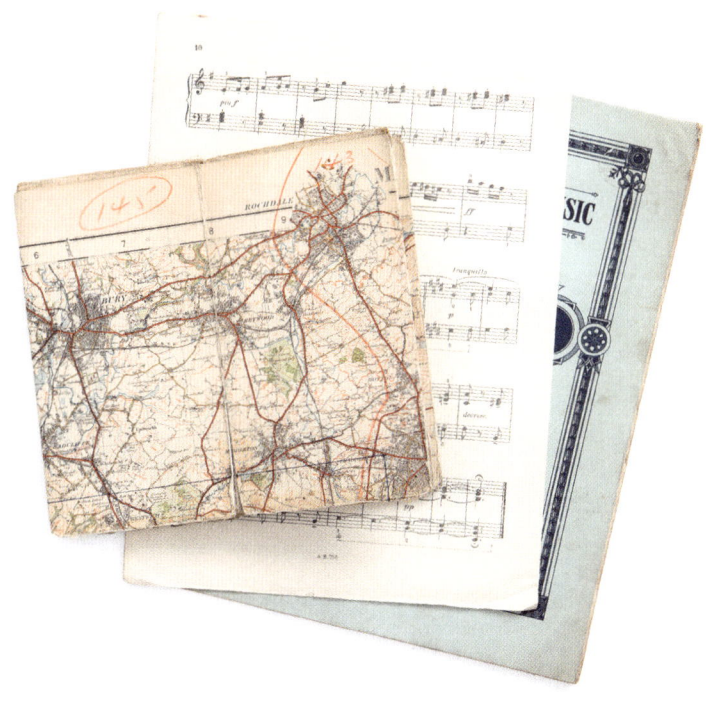

# Choosing what to print

## Flowers and leaves

Plants are the perfect subjects for cyanotype prints.
Everywhere we look, from urban centres to country
fields, we are surrounded by botanical inspiration.
Pick fresh plants or flowers and place them directly
onto your print for an ethereal, soft result.

Once you start exploring the plants and flowers
around you with cyanotypes in mind, you will be amazed
by the variety and beauty of the unique forms to be found.
Take delight in the detail of a fern or in the lacy patterns
of a well-munched leaf. The inspiration is infinite.

For historical inspiration, look up Anna Atkins,
the nineteenth-century amateur botanist who became
known as the first published female photographer.
She used her fascination and skill with the cyanotype
technique in order to better understand the plant
life she studied.

## Pressed flowers

Pressing flowers and leaves preserves your botanical
subjects for longer and allows you to use them again.
Using pressed plants will also give a more crisp and
detailed effect in your prints (see opposite). If you don't
press your botanicals, you'll find that the piece will have
wilted and shrivelled in a short time. This can add to the
magic of cyanotypes, where every print is unique, but
if you find a particularly beautiful specimen, you might
want to re-use it.

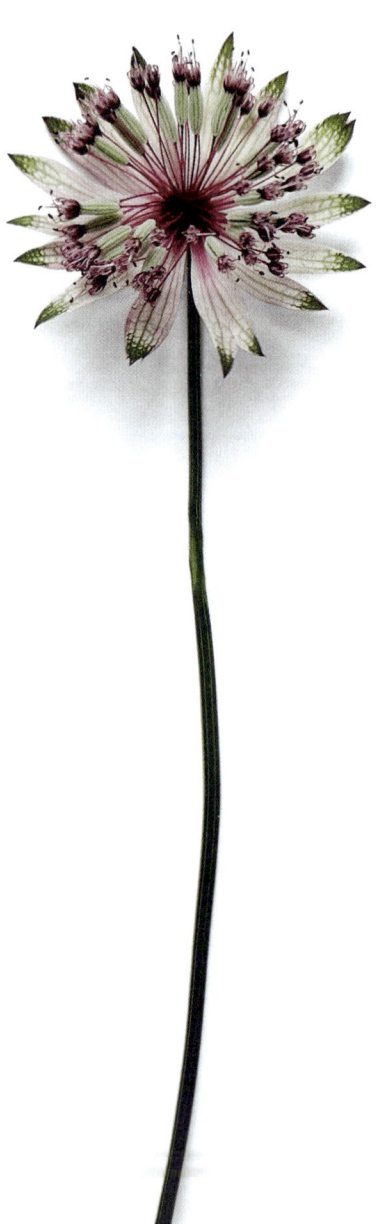

## Out and about

I take a sketchbook out with me on walks to press the leaves and flowers that catch my eye as I go. If I press (and dry) the specimens while I'm out foraging, I find that I can keep what I've collected to use in my prints. If I don't press what I find right away, I'm usually disappointed by the time I get home, as that perfect botanical specimen will have wilted before I can use it.

**Below, left:** A pressed Astrantia flower gives a crisp image when captured in a cyanotype.

**Below right:** When freshly picked flowers are used for cyanotypes there is a softer effect.

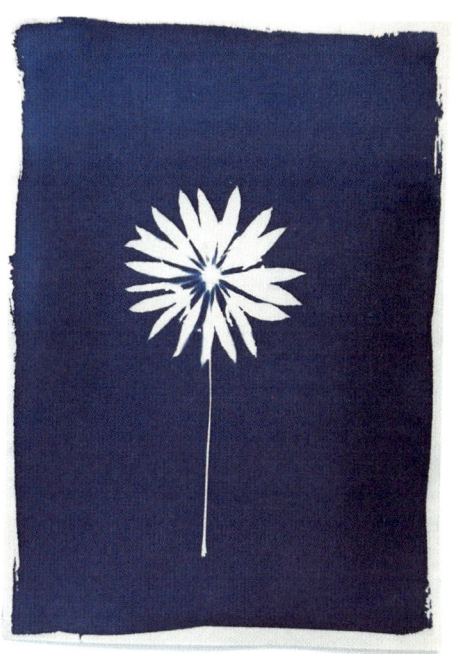

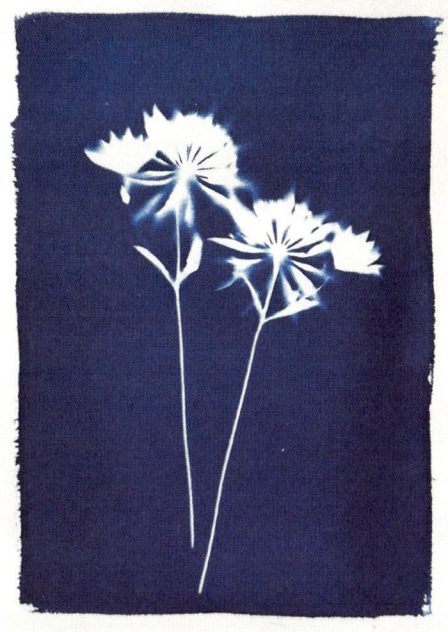

# How to press flowers

To press the plants I have gathered, I use sheets of blotting paper with layers of cardboard in a press. You can buy flower presses from art shops and online but these tend to be not much larger than A4. If, for example, you want to preserve big, beautiful ferns, you might want to consider building your own press with two sheets of wood or MDF. Simply drill holes at each corner to insert coach bolts and wing nuts and you can make a press as large as you like.

The other option is to use a hardback sketchbook – you can press your specimens between the pages and use strong clips to create the necessary pressure to preserve the botanicals inside.

Some botanicals work better for pressing than others. As a rule of thumb, the flatter the original specimen, the easier it will be to preserve it.

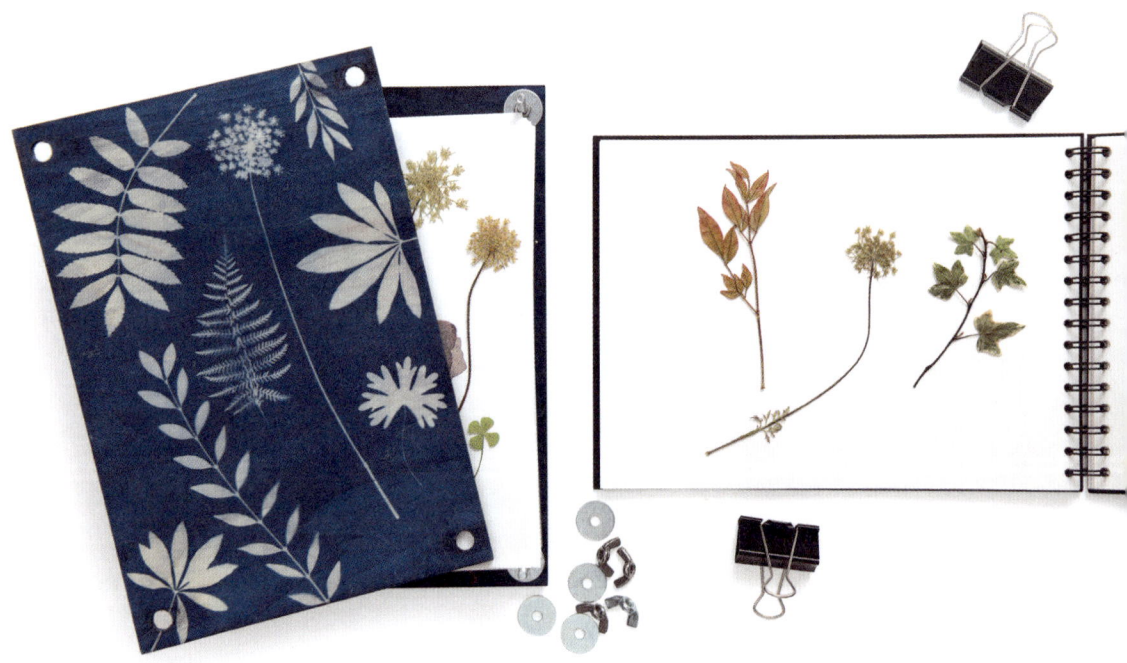

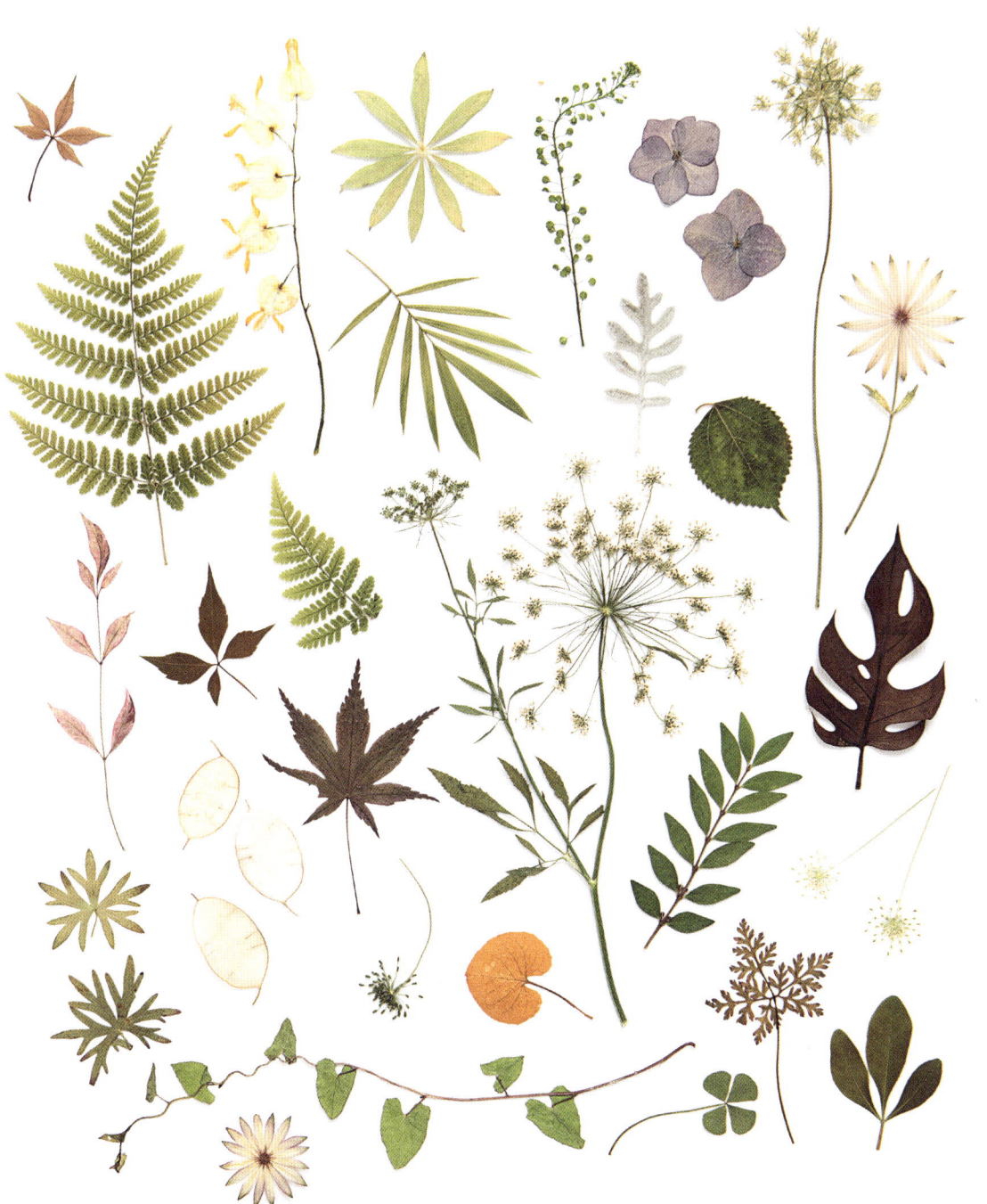

# Found objects

When you look around you, what do you see that has potential to create a cyanotype print? Whatever you place on your print will block the light, and the flatter the object, the crisper the resulting image will be. You might want to experiment with antique lace or keys, old jewellery or bits and pieces from the tool box or the cutlery drawer.

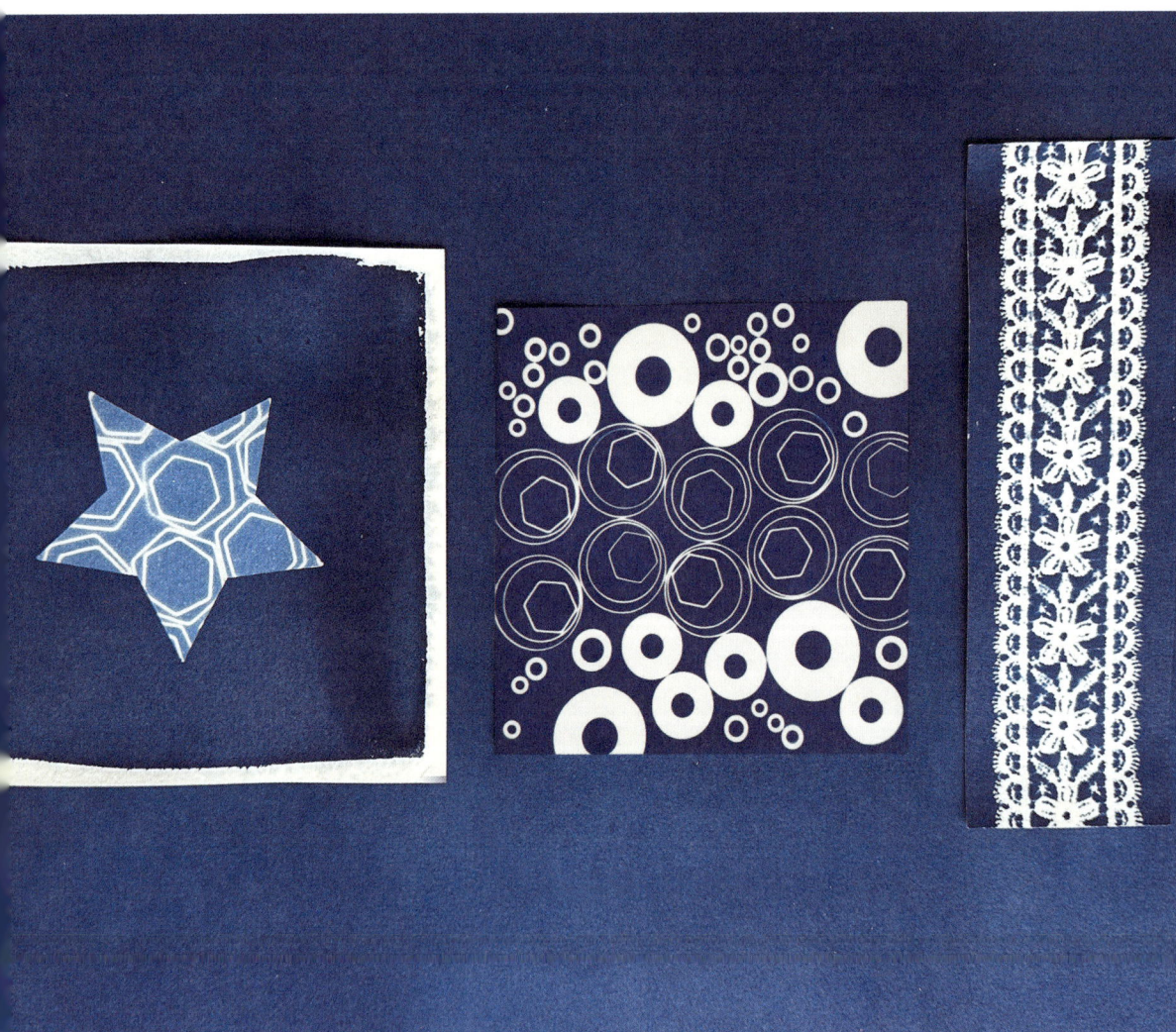

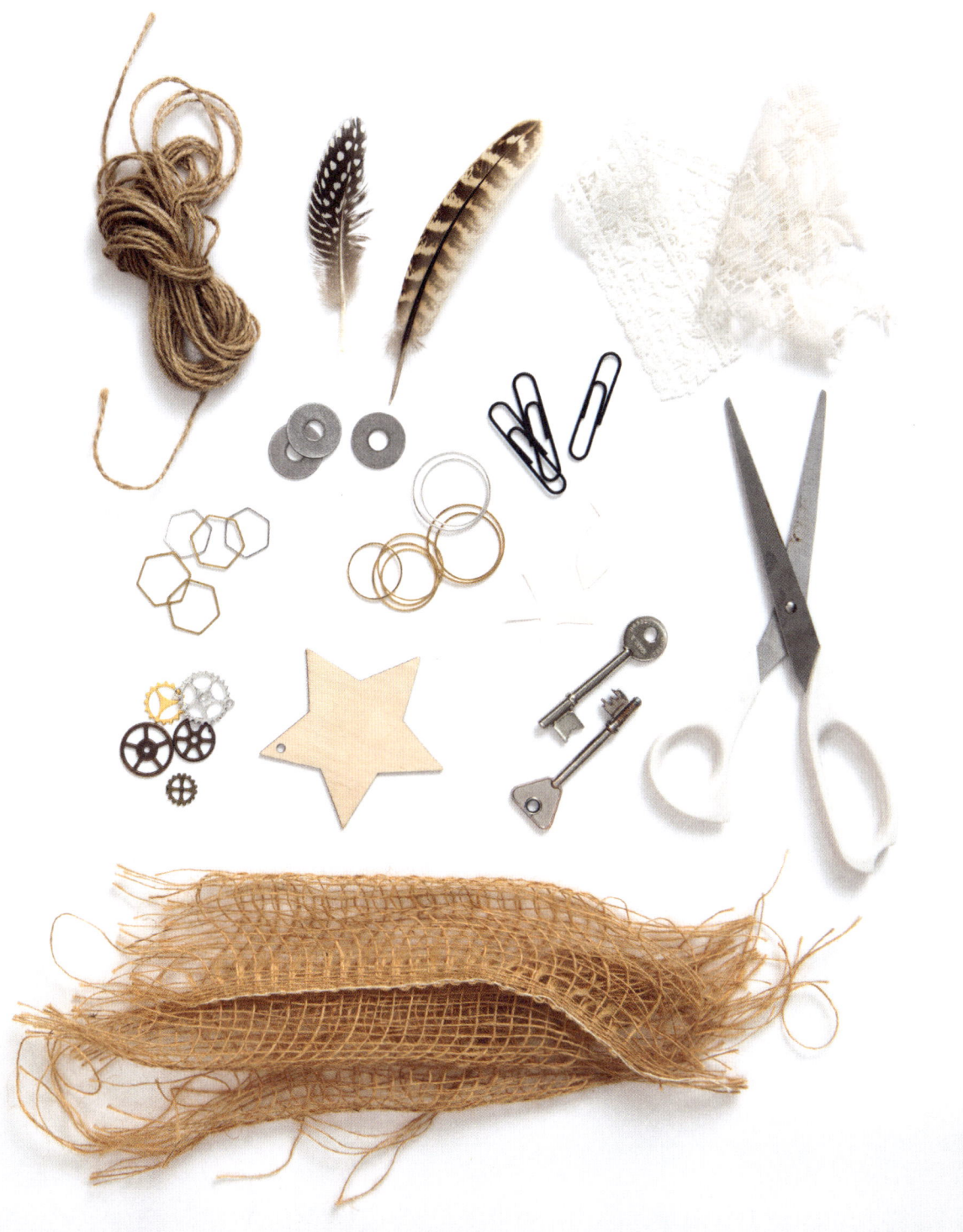

## Backgrounds and textures

Anything that blocks the light can create a cyanotype print including mesh, grids, paper packaging or even patterned tissue papers. Have a look around you to see what would create an interesting texture or abstract print. These can be used by themselves, or you can layer them up, as we will explore on page 58.

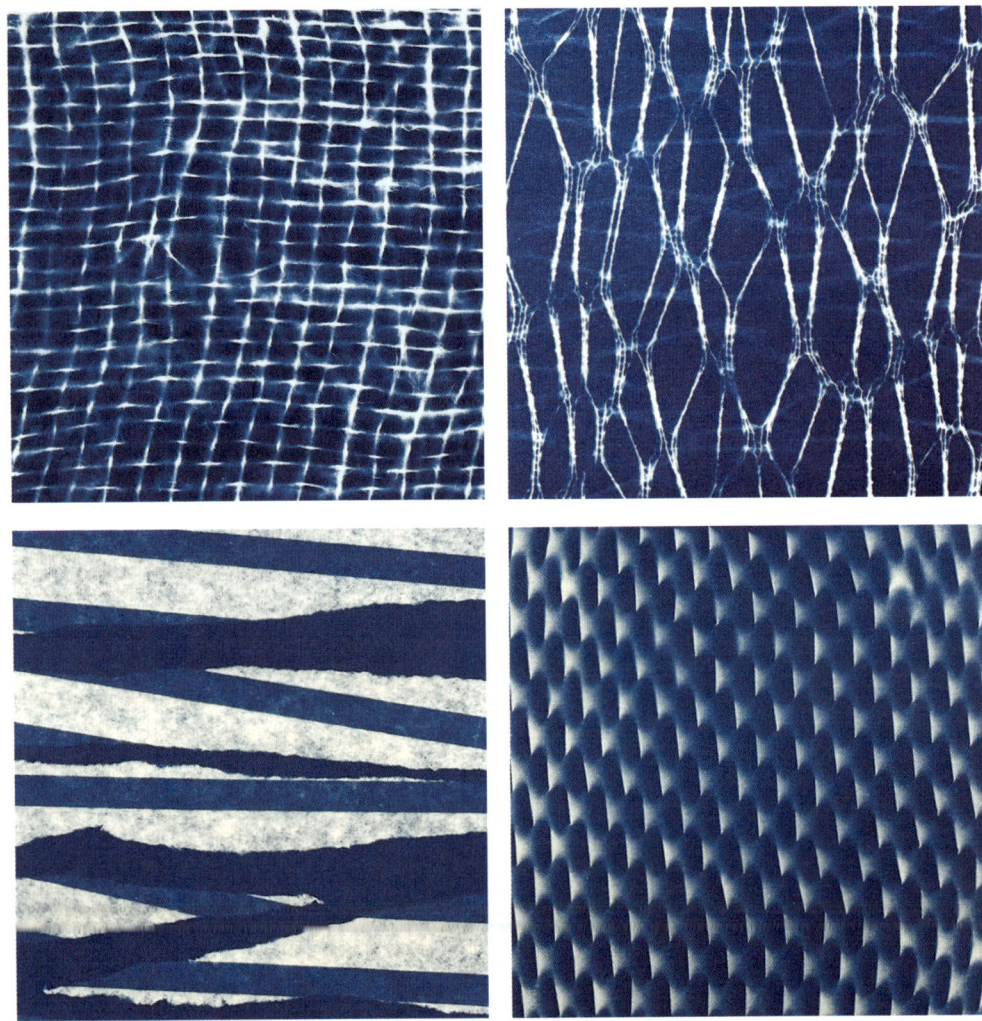

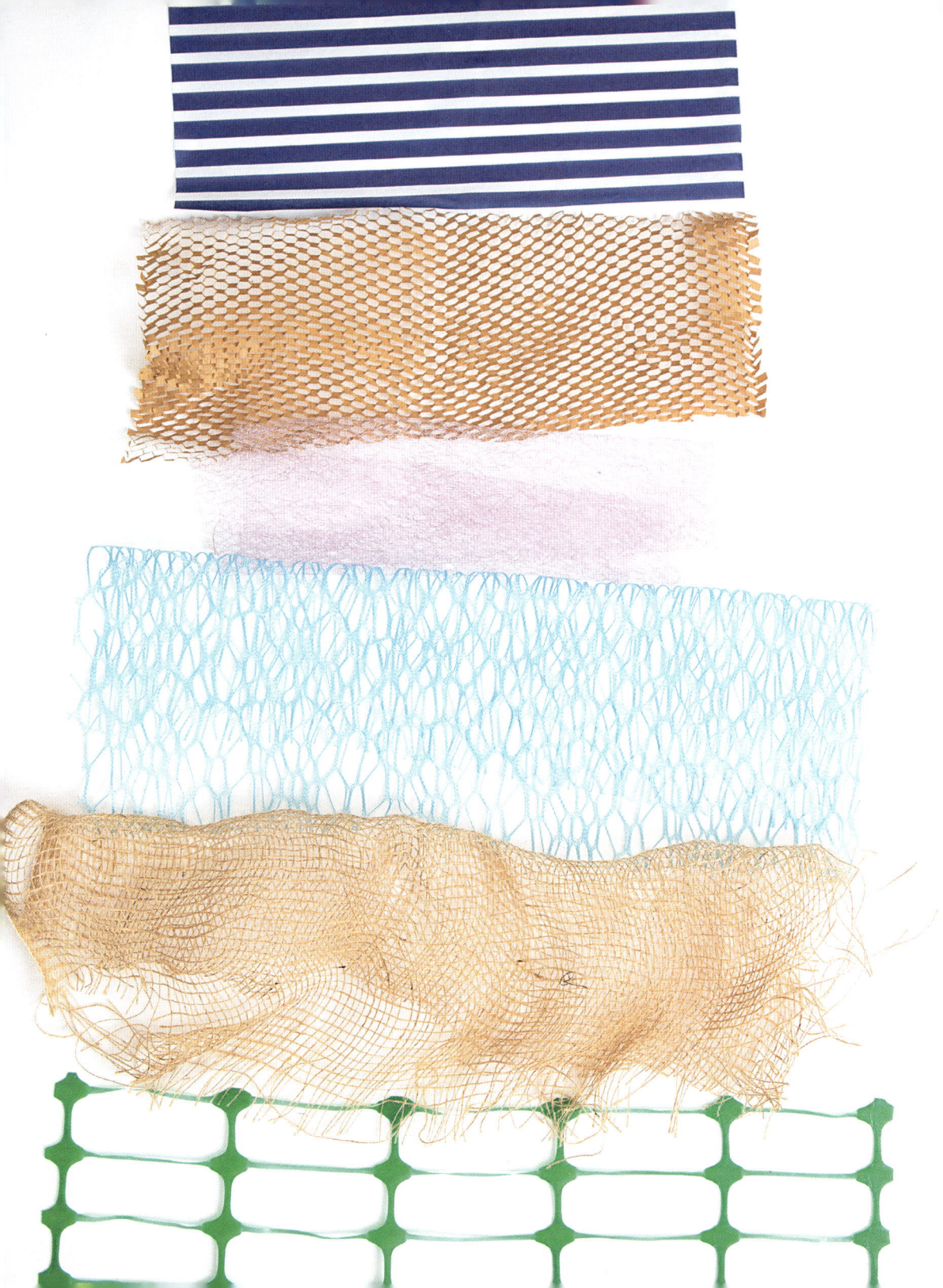

# Building a composition

The simple elegance of a beautiful leaf can create a striking composition all by itself but, as you gain more confidence in the cyanotype process, you'll probably want to experiment more with your prints. As you familiarize yourself with how the technique works and how the objects you choose create different results, think about how you can develop your designs. One method is to lay out your subjects to create patterns.

You can use a circular shape such as a plate to guide you in a wreath design or arrange your objects to fill the whole of your print surface. Don't feel confined to the edges of the paper or fabric you are printing on. Explore negative space to create a dramatic composition.

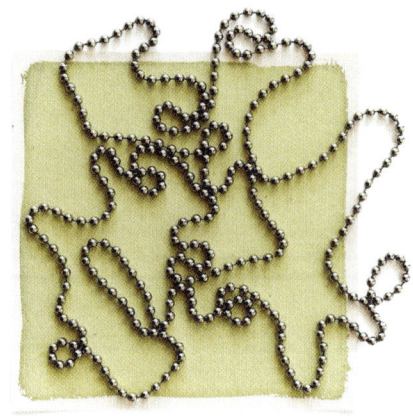

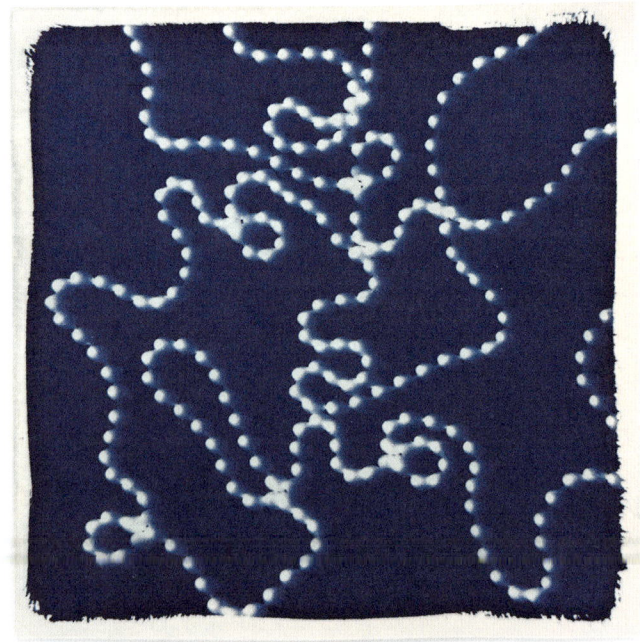

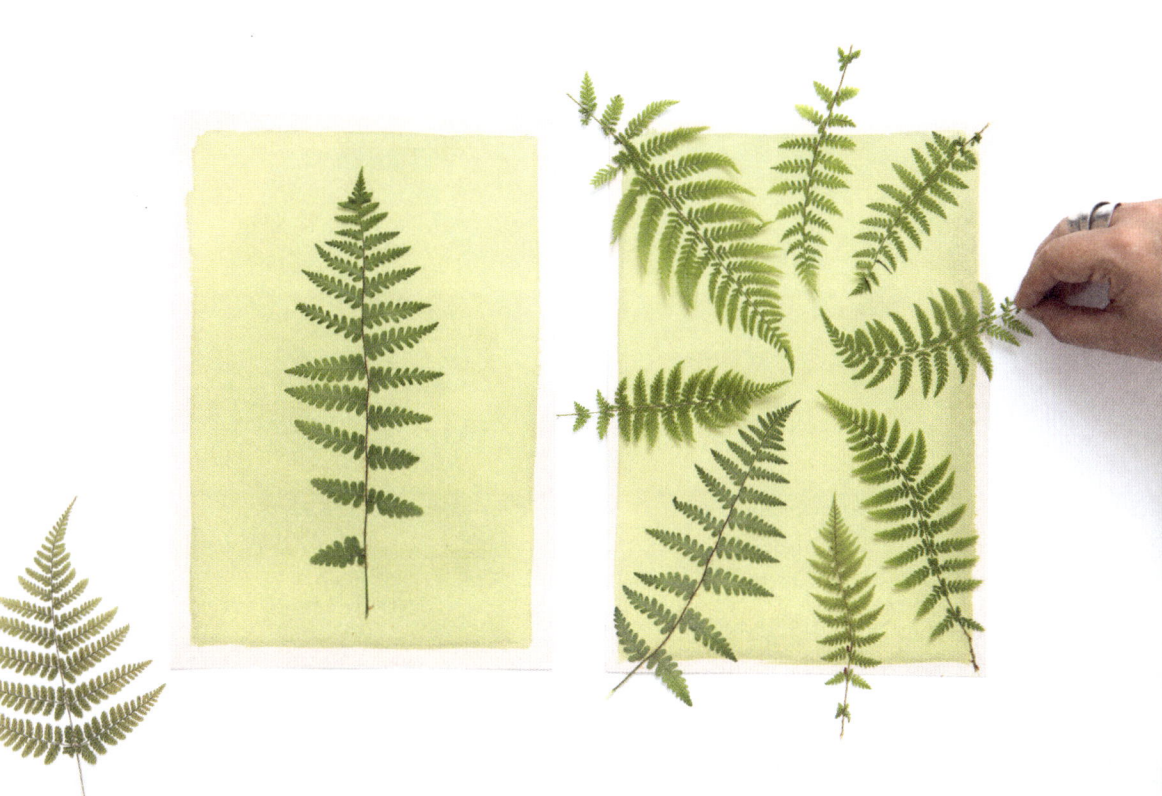

Are you going to make a simple print of a single object or are you going to arrange a more complicated composition with a number of objects? Move them around the paper to imagine your finished print. Do you want to contain your objects within your coated area or do you want your objects to fall outside of that area? Are you looking for patterns or will you let the object speak for itself?

# Techniques
# and effects

The cyanotype process is a simple one but there are plenty of creative ways in which you can push the technique further.

# Playing with application

The thing to remember when making cyanotypes is that there is no definitive right or wrong way at any stage of making the print. How you coat the print is part of your creative process. You might want to experiment by splashing the emulsion on, dabbing at the wet emulsion with a paper towel or splashing some water on to dilute it in places. The cyanotype technique is the perfect technique to ask yourself 'I wonder what would happen if...?'

Try different types of brushes to achieve different effects when applying emulsion. Do you want a very thin, even coating? Consider a foam brush. Do you want to achieve freely brushed edges where you can see the brush marks? Try a Japanese hake-style brush. Do you want to paint a silhouette of something like the shape of an animal or a circle? Use a regular paintbrush. You can use any form of tool to apply your emulsion and have some fun with mark making to see what happens. Opposite are a few variations of application that result in different outcomes.

**Opposite:**

**1.** Emulsion dabbed on with a sponge to create texture.

**2.** Emulsion applied with a Japanese-style hake brush to create obvious brushed edges.

**3.** Emulsion coated evenly over the entire surface of the print using a sponge brush.

**4.** Emulsion applied with a paint brush to create a neat circle.

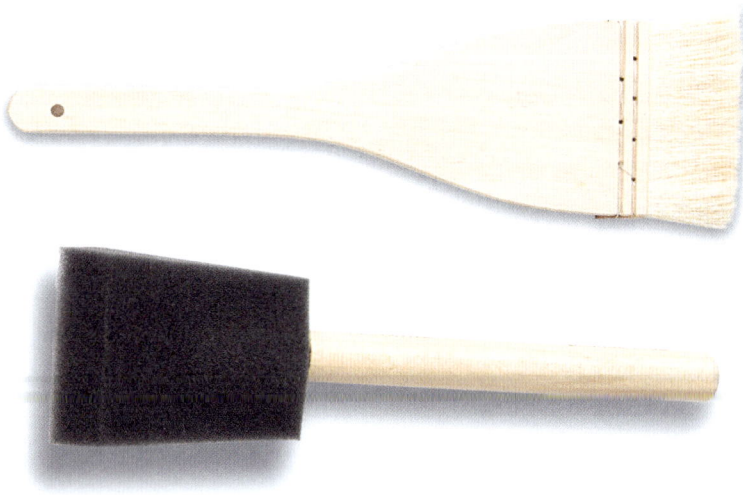

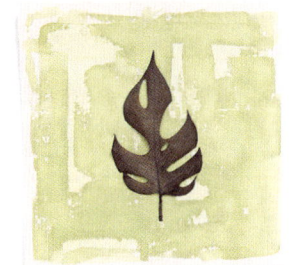
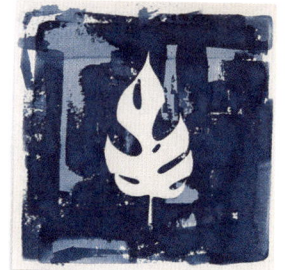

**1**

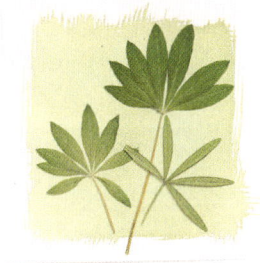
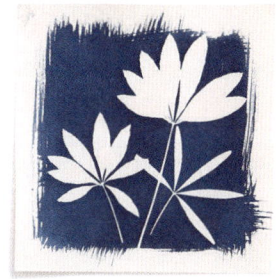

**2**

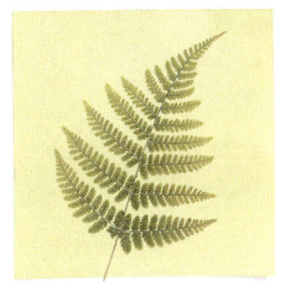
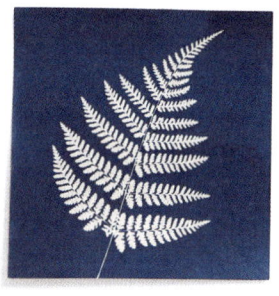

**3**

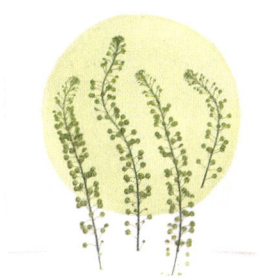
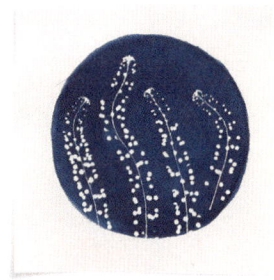

**4**

# Toning with tannins

The striking shades of blue and white are what makes a traditional cyanotype print so recognizable, but you can achieve a different colour using tea, coffee or anything that contains tannins, including tannic acid.

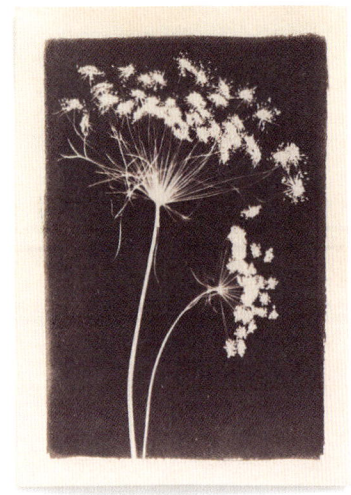

**1.** Choose the cyanotype print you'd like to turn a shade of brown. This step is irreversible so you might want to practice on a sample print. Note that the darker the shade of your original print, the darker the shade of brown you will achieve after dyeing.

**2.** Before you create your brown print you need to bleach the original blue one. Fill a washing-up bowl or tray with tap water and dissolve a few tablespoons of soda crystals in the water. (Soda crystals are easily available from the supermarket.)

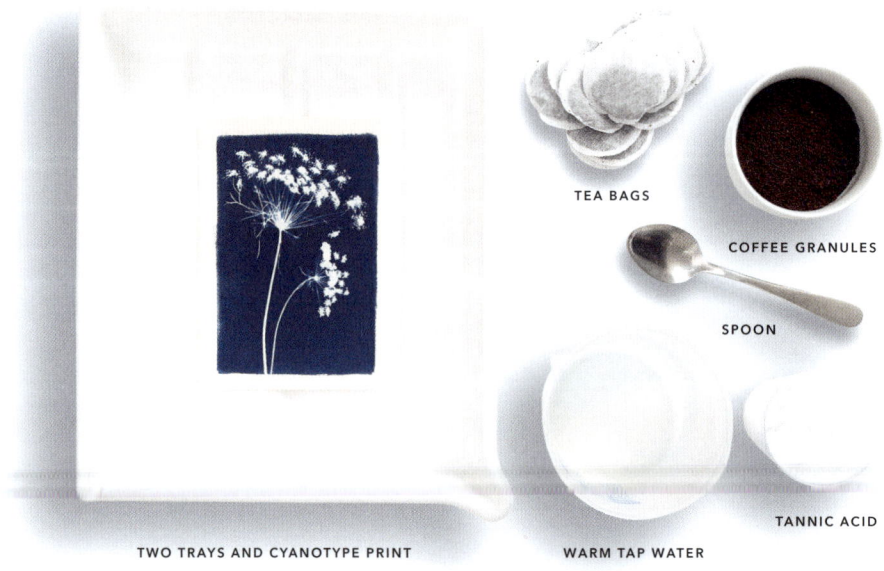

TEA BAGS

COFFEE GRANULES

SPOON

TWO TRAYS AND CYANOTYPE PRINT

WARM TAP WATER

TANNIC ACID

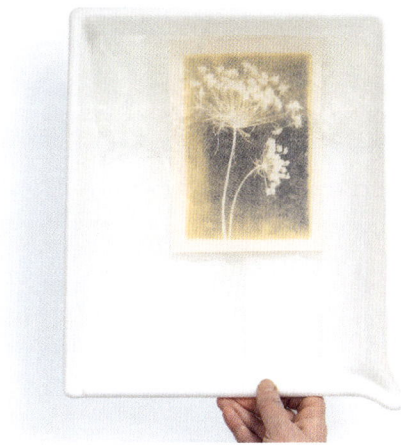

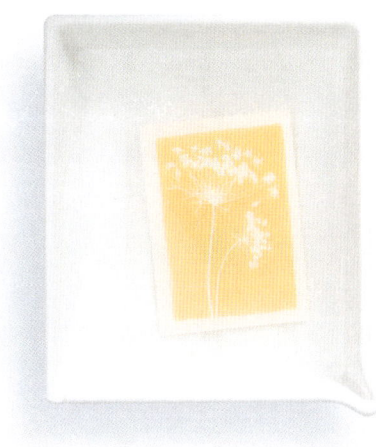

**3.** Place the blue print in your bleach solution, and it will immediately start changing to a shade of yellow. Agitating the solution slightly will speed it up a bit.

**4.** You should get a bright yellow after about five minutes. You can't over-bleach it.

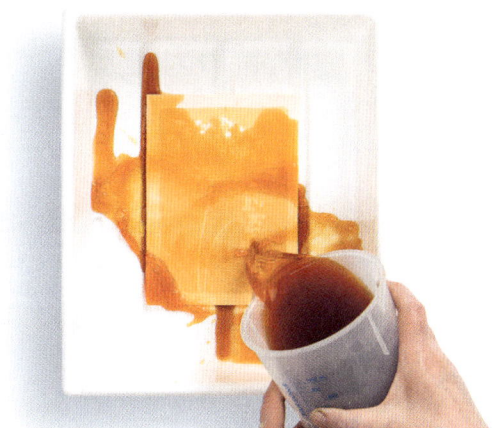

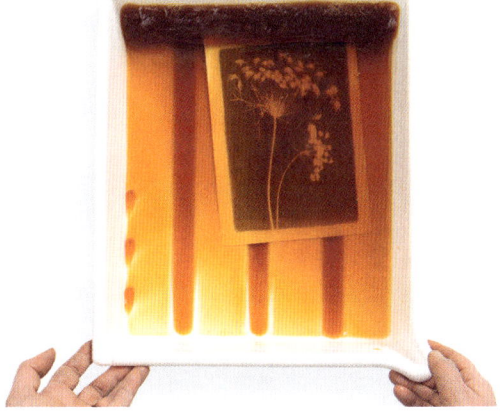

**5.** Next make a strong tannin solution using several tea bags and/or coffee mixed with warm water. You will need a strong concentration of tannins so experiment with the amounts. You don't need to use tannic acid as well but it will give you a deeper colour and quicker result if that's what you are after. Place your bleached print in a new tray and pour in your solution.

**6.** The aim is for your bleached yellow print to change to a shade of brown after you've immersed it for several minutes. The stronger your original solution the quicker you will achieve a dark brown. Once you have your desired tone, remove the print from the tray, rinse and peg out to dry.

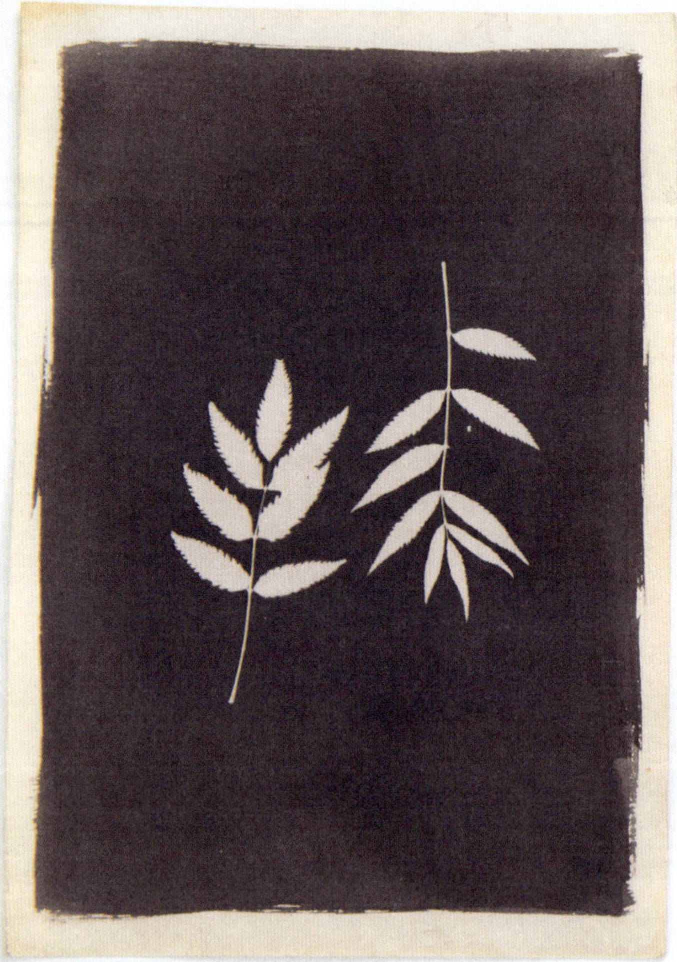

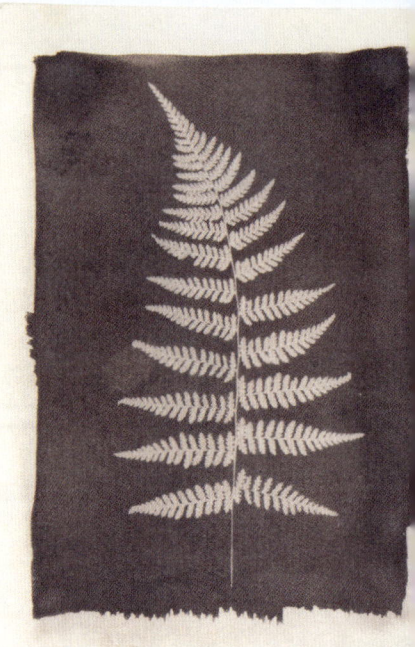
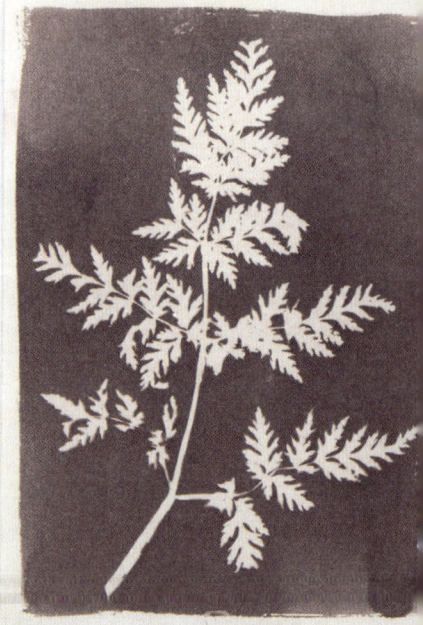

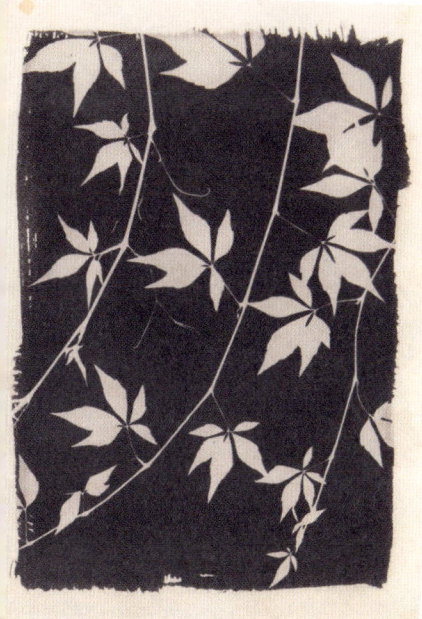
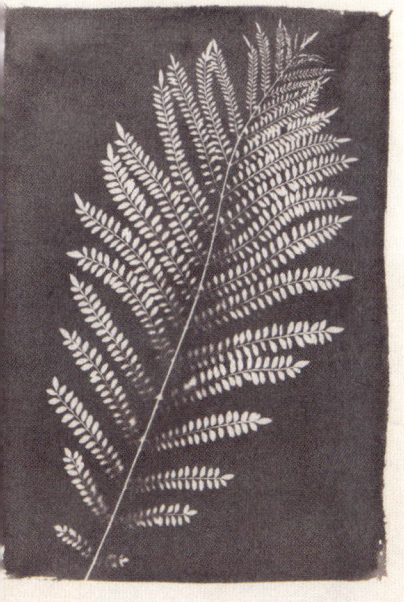
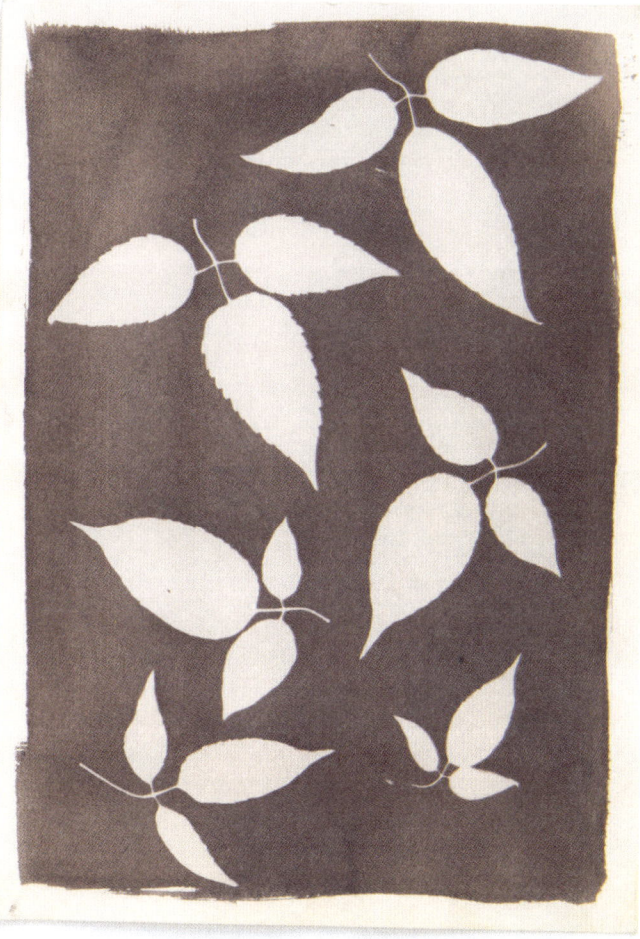

# Wet cyanotypes

The cyanotype technique is charmingly unpredictable at the best of times but adding extra elements to the paper while it is still wet creates interesting new textures and takes the process to whole new levels of serendipity. You can create interesting textural effects with dishwashing liquid bubbles, salt, vinegar and plastic wrap, and turmeric can add a flash of orange or yellow to your finished print.

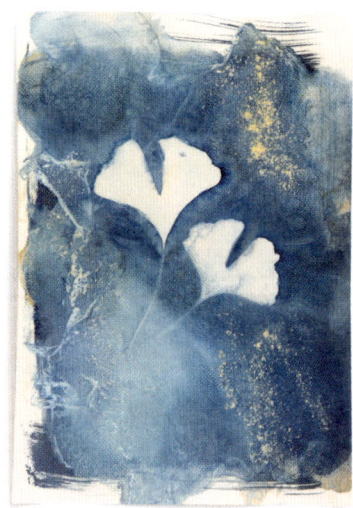

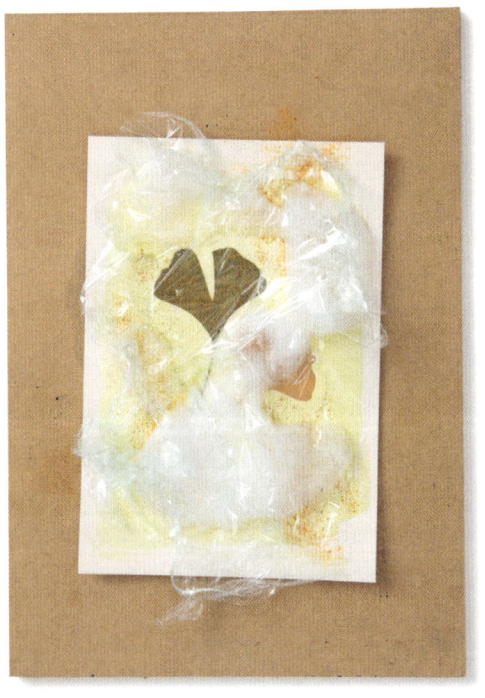

**1.** Paint the emulsion directly on to your paper or fabric and place your subject on top while it is still wet. Add various elements, such as a splash of white vinegar, a dash of salt, some dishwashing liquid foam or a sprinkle of turmeric. There is no right or wrong way to do this.

**2.** Cover the print in scrunched-up plastic wrap to add yet more texture and gently cover with the Perspex before placing outside or under a UV lamp. You don't need to clip down your Perspex as you want to preserve the textures created by the bubbles and the plastic wrap.

**3.** Expose your print. Longer exposures tend to work better with wet cyanotypes.

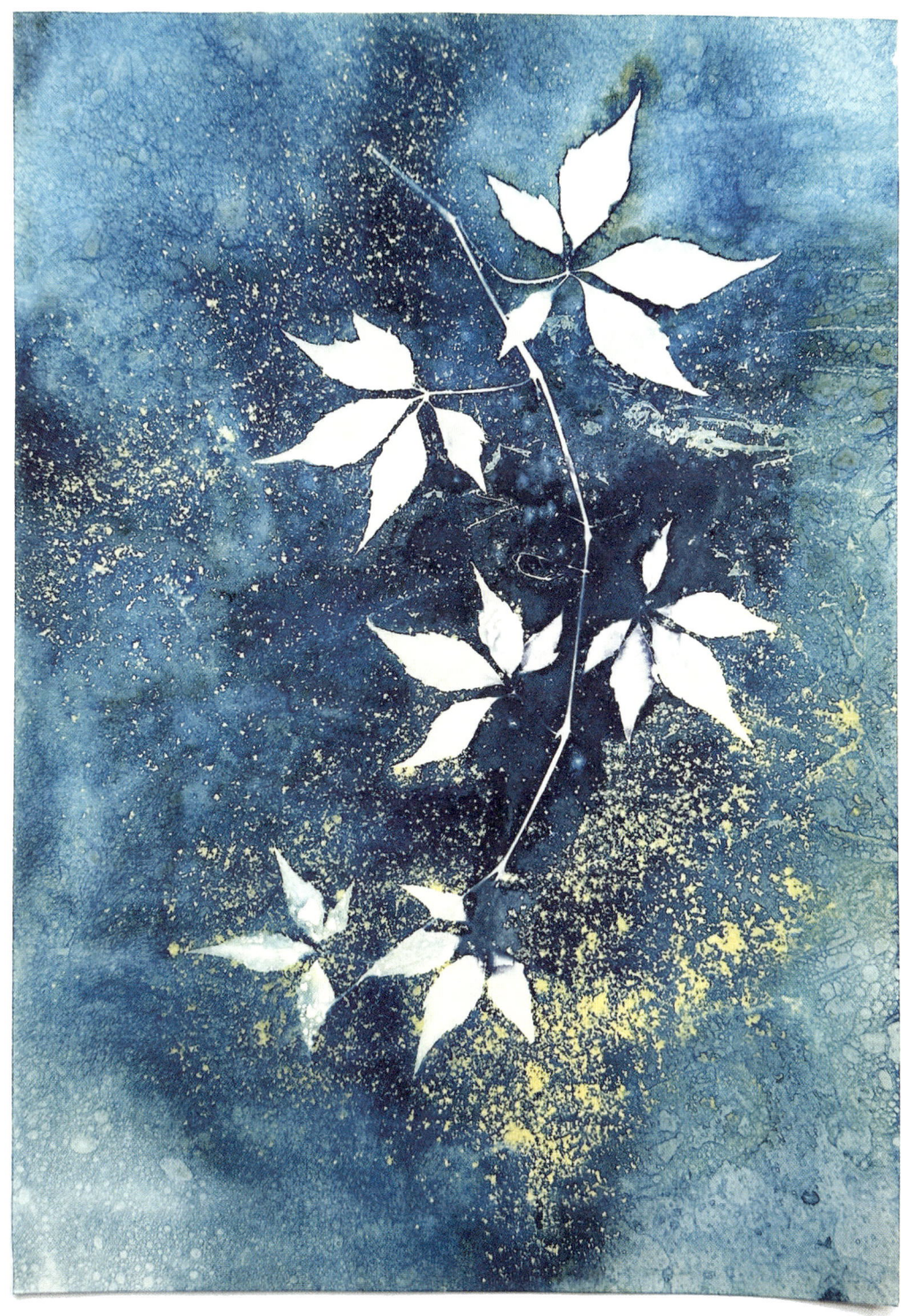

# Photographic negatives

The possibilities are endless when working with photographic images, from patterns and portraits to landscapes and flowers and everything else in between. You don't need any specialist camera equipment – I mainly use images that I've taken on my phone – but you will need a printer.

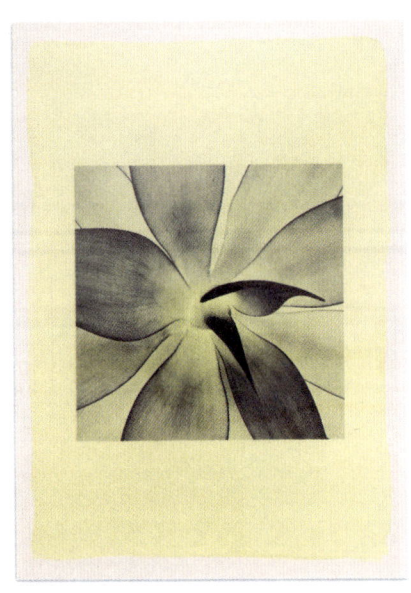

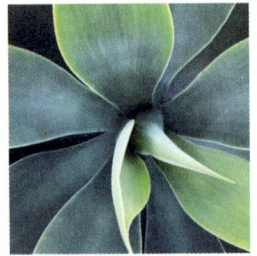

1. Choose an image that has enough contrast to work well as a cyanotype print.

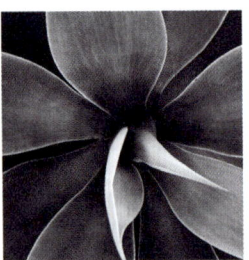

2. Using Photoshop or free software available online, convert the image to black and white.

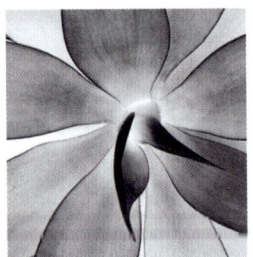

3. Next invert the image so that it becomes a negative. This is the image that you are going to place on top of your prepared paper or fabric print to create your design.

4. Print out your image on a sheet of acetate. Make sure you buy the correct acetates for your printer – either ink jet or laser transparency film depending on the printer you are using – and allow the ink to dry before using. Ink jet printers tend to give denser blacks which are better at blocking the light.

5. Place the transparency on your coated surface and cover with your Perspex or glass sheet to ensure that your image is as detailed as possible before exposing it. You might need to do a test print first to ensure that the exposure time is correct (see page 15).

6. Rinse in a tray of fresh water until the chemicals have washed out and peg up to dry or pat dry with paper towels.

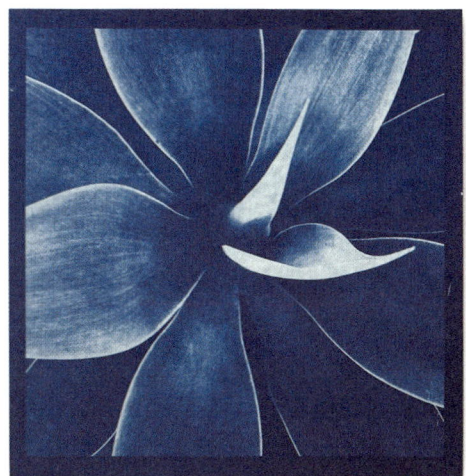

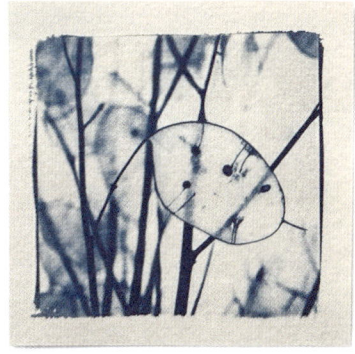

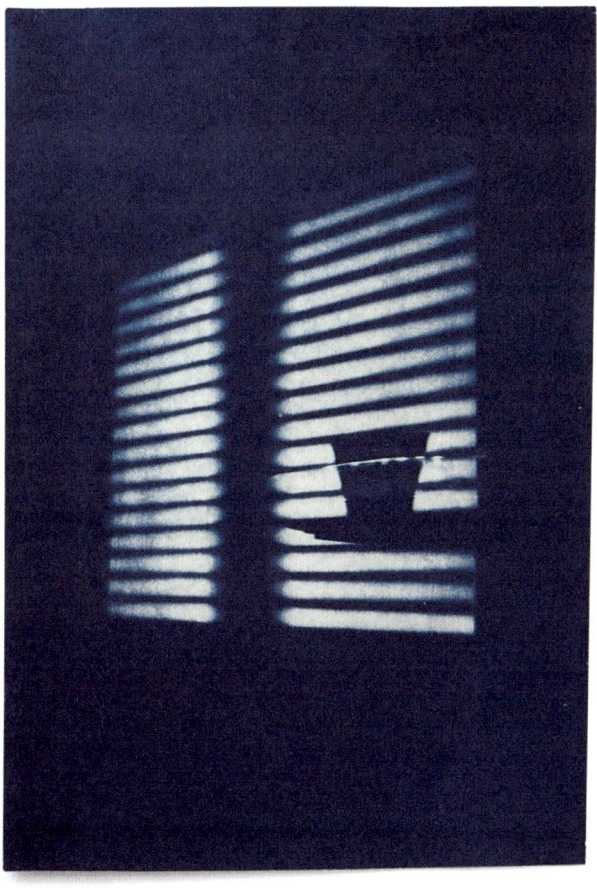

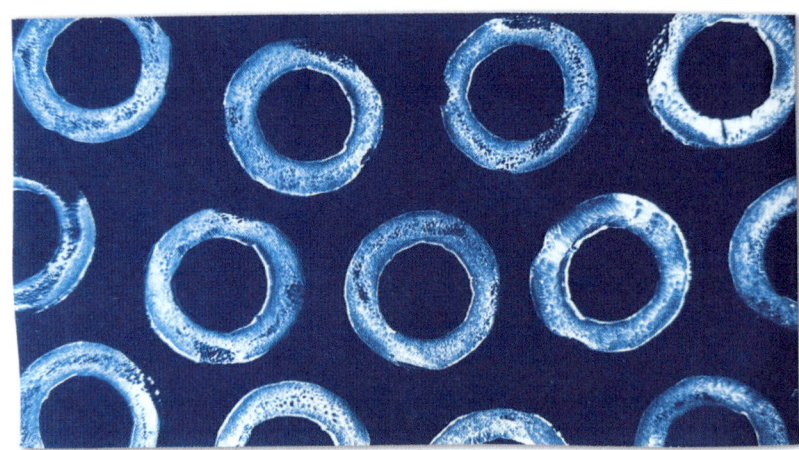

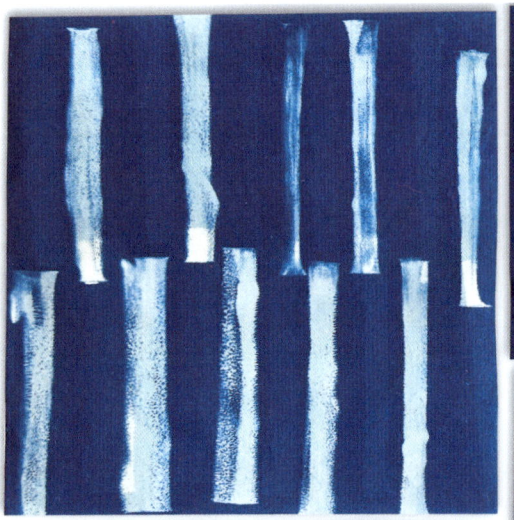

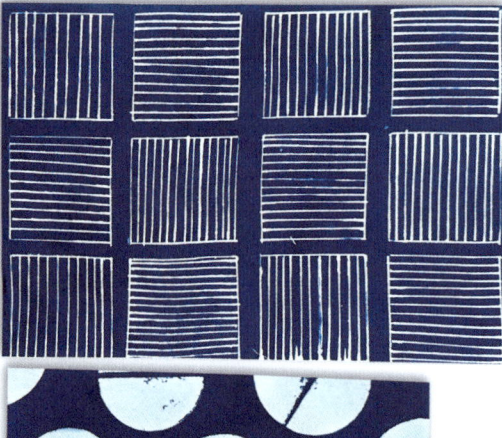

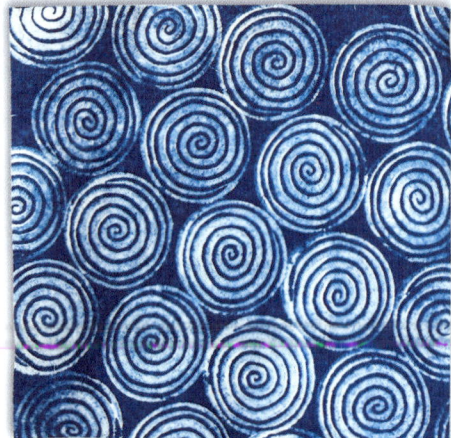

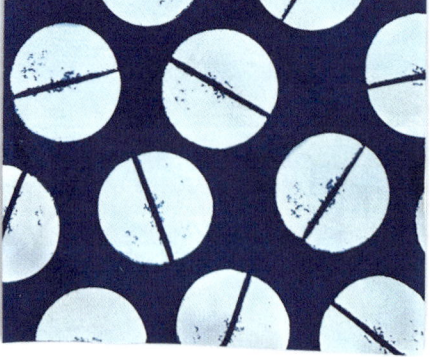

# Mark making on acetate

We have already looked at creating negatives for cyanotypes using photographic images printed on acetate sheets, but you can also draw or paint directly on to a sheet of acetate, and then use that as a design. As long as the pen or the paint is thick enough to block the light, you can draw or write anything you wish to create patterns or artworks.

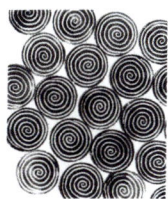 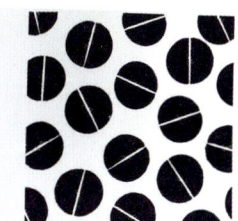

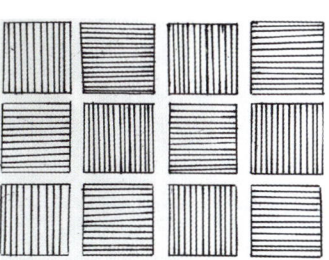 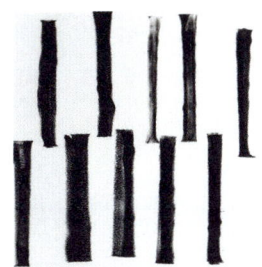 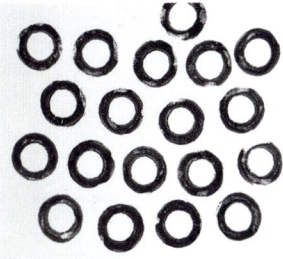

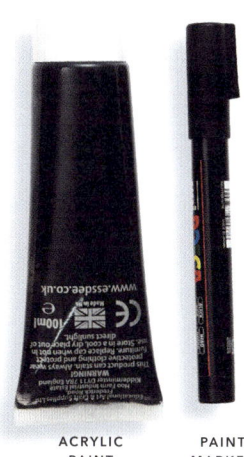 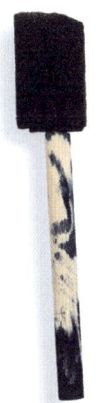 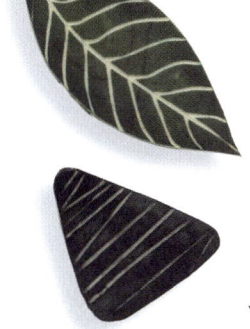 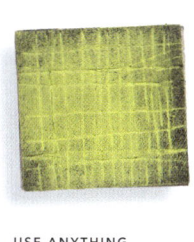

USE ANYTHING
YOU WOULD LIKE TO
CREATE PATTERNS

ACRYLIC
PAINT

PAINT
MARKER

SPONGE
BRUSH

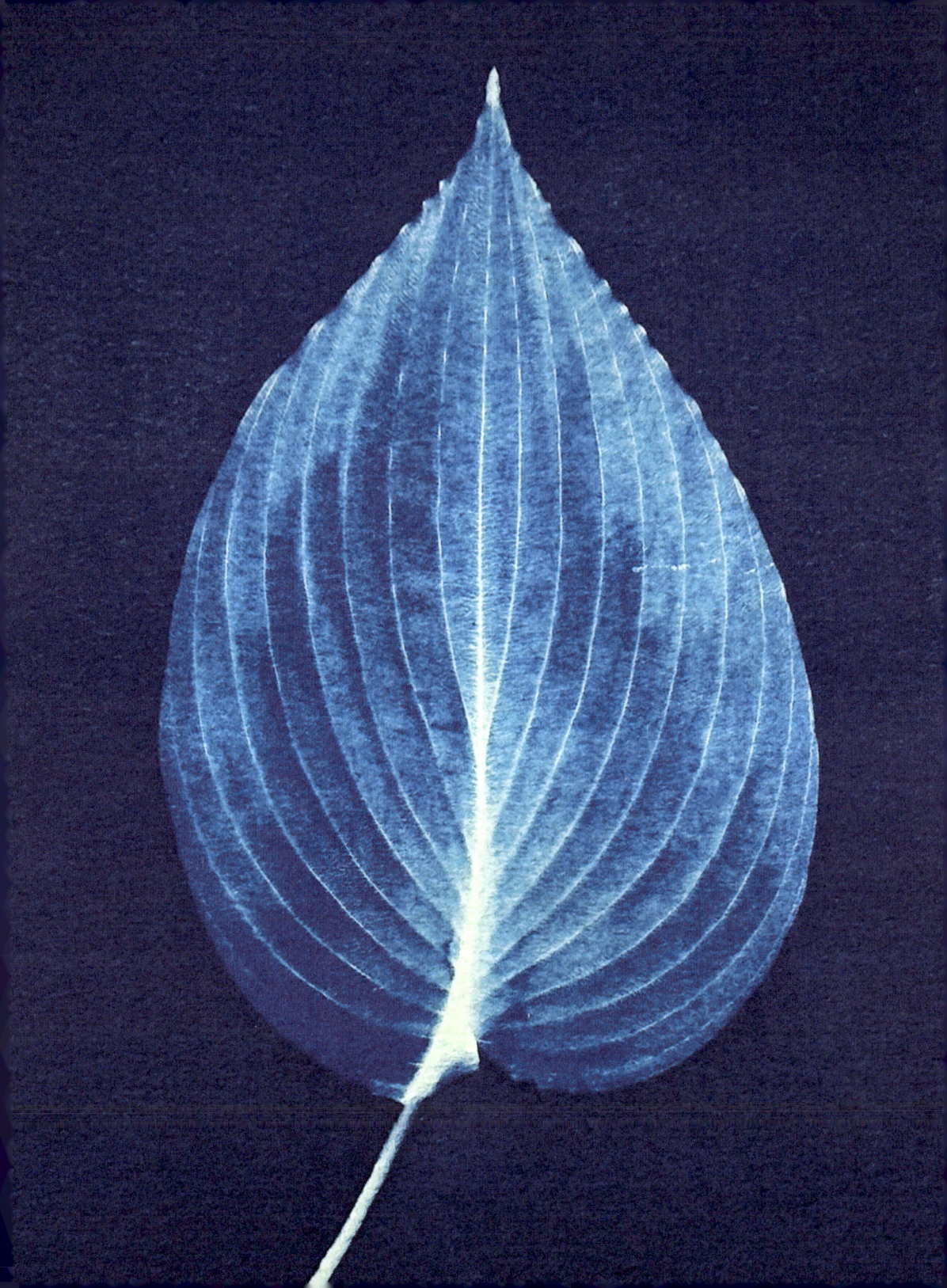

# Long exposures to create X-ray effects

A simple cyanotype exposure results in a white silhouette on a blue background, but it's possible to expose your object on your print for much longer. What happens if you expose your print for five hours, for example? It's best to use an object that isn't too delicate – the longer you expose a fine object, the more you will lose the detail. Start with bold-shaped leaves that aren't too thick and expose for at least an hour to see what you get. You might need to expose even longer to really get that X-ray effect where you can see all the delicate veins within the leaf or flower.

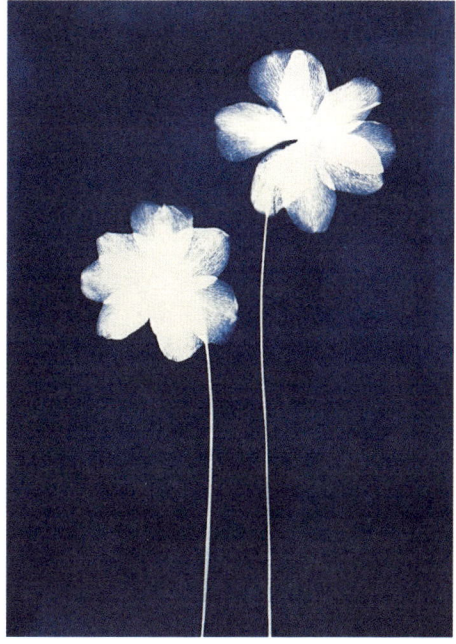

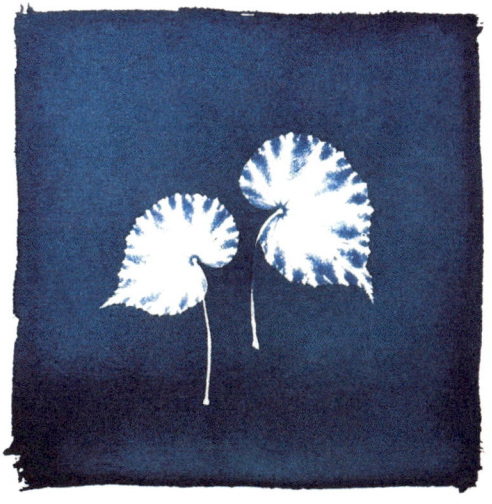

# Using shadows in exposures

Shadows are fantastic to play with when using the sun to expose your print. When the sun isn't directly overhead, it will cast a shadow, as long as the object you're using on the surface of your print isn't flat – think bulkier flowers like tulips or objects like vases or bottles.

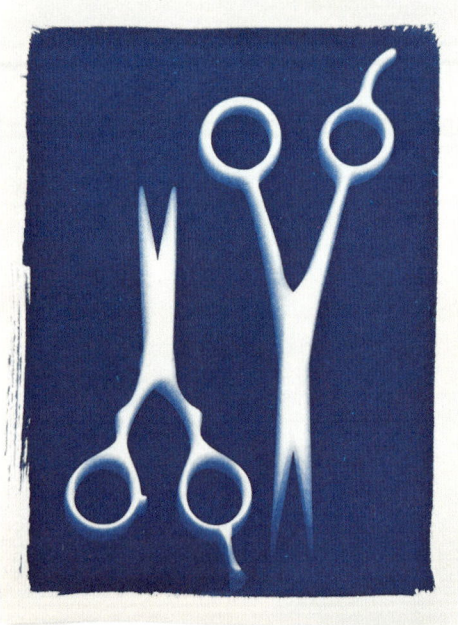

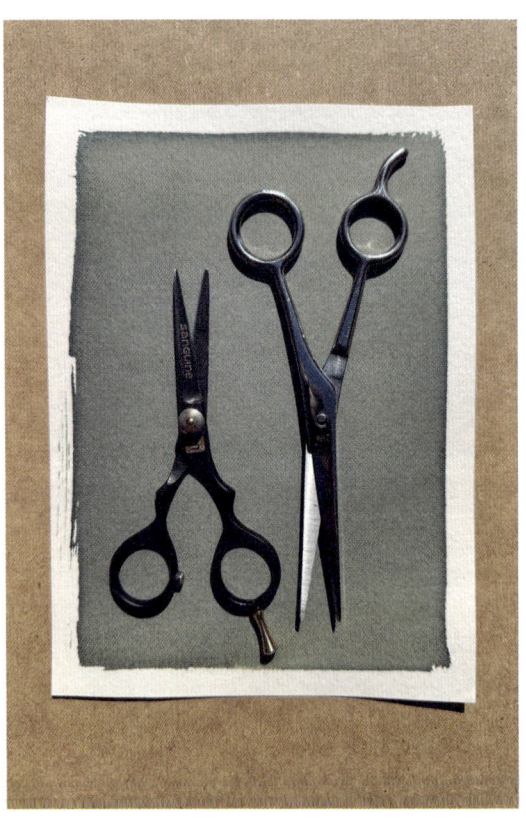

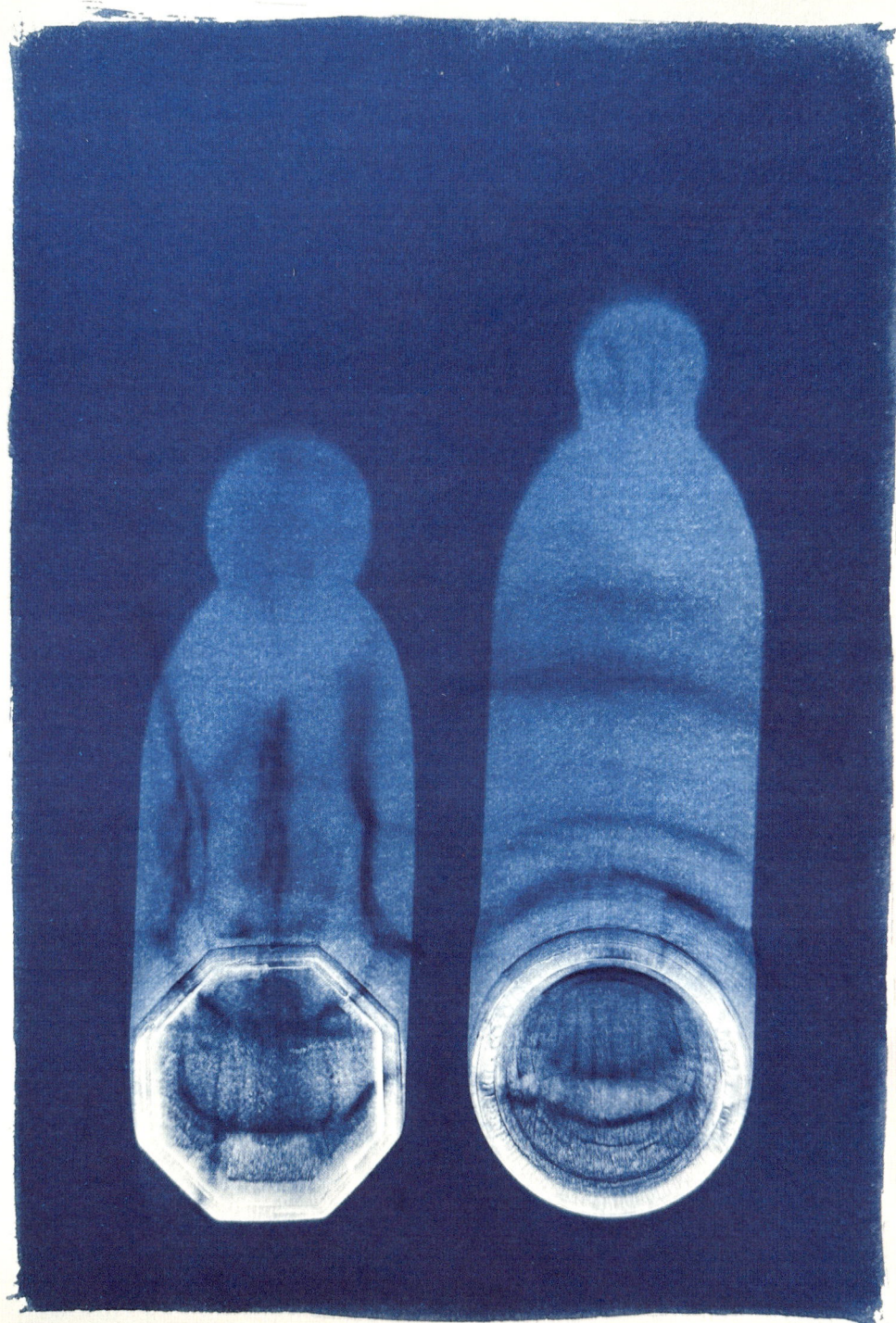

# Multiple exposures

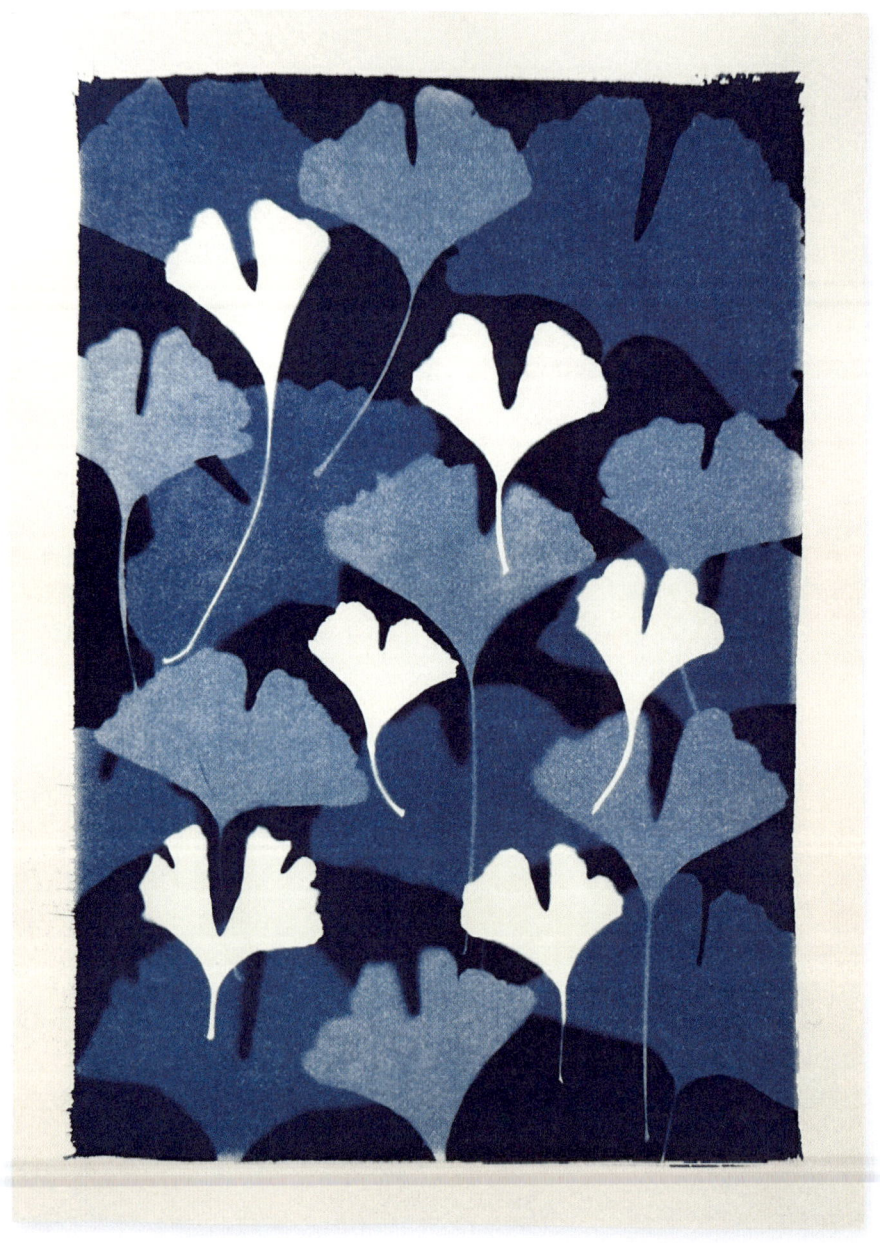

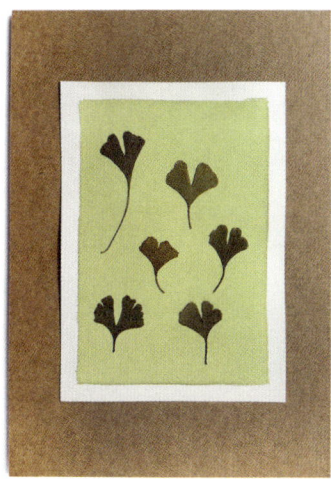

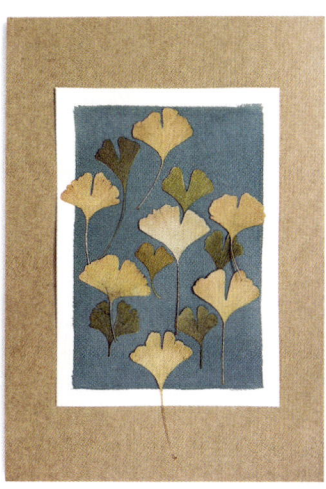

**1.** Plan your composition starting with the smallest objects. Arrange them on the surface of the paper, cover with the Perspex and 'pre-expose' your print. You don't want to expose your print for too long at this stage, just enough to allow the emulsion to start to turn blue.

**2.** Remove the print from the sun/UV light and lift off the Perspex carefully to add your larger leaves on top of and around your smaller leaves. Take care not to move your first layer of small leaves as you don't want any light to get under those. Put the Perspex back and expose your print as you would normally.

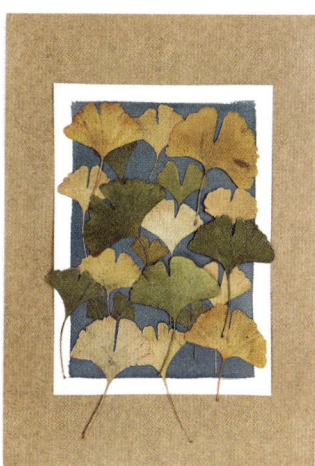

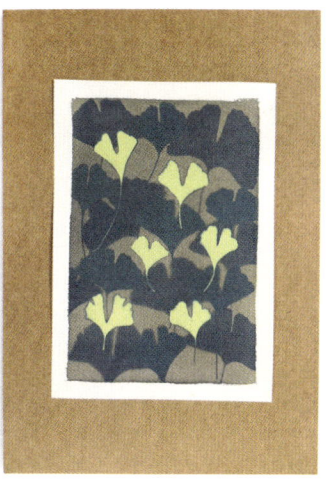

**3.** The resulting print should have an additional shade of blue. You could continue with a third layer of leaves if you choose to.

**4.** When you remove the leaves you will see the variations in tone on the print. Rinse and dry as normal.

# Moving objects mid-exposure

On page 58, we talked about making multiple exposures in order to achieve different levels of blue in the resulting print. Try starting with a short 'pre-exposure' but, instead of adding new objects, remove the objects you've already used, and then expose the print again so that you have a double impression of the same objects.

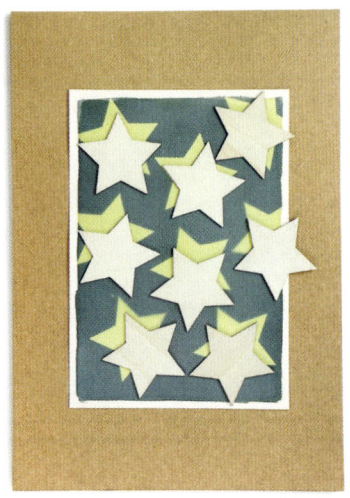

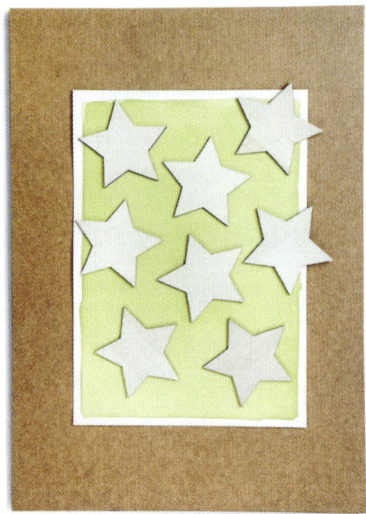

**1.** Place your objects on your coated paper. Bear in mind that you're going to be moving them after an initial exposure so you might want to allow room for your objects to move into. Cover with Perspex and clamp to get the best details. Expose your print for a short while. The length of exposure depends on the strength of your UV source (sun or UV lamp).

**2.** Bring your print back inside or remove from under your lamp and move the objects slightly. You don't really want to move your objects too much as the aim is to create a shadow. Cover with the Perspex and this time expose for longer as this is your end exposure.

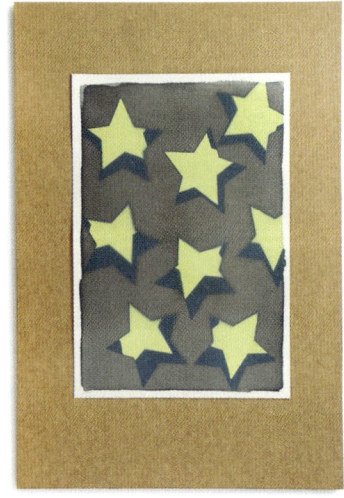

**3.** Remove your objects, rinse and dry. Hopefully you will see a clear shadow in a paler blue where you have moved your objects.

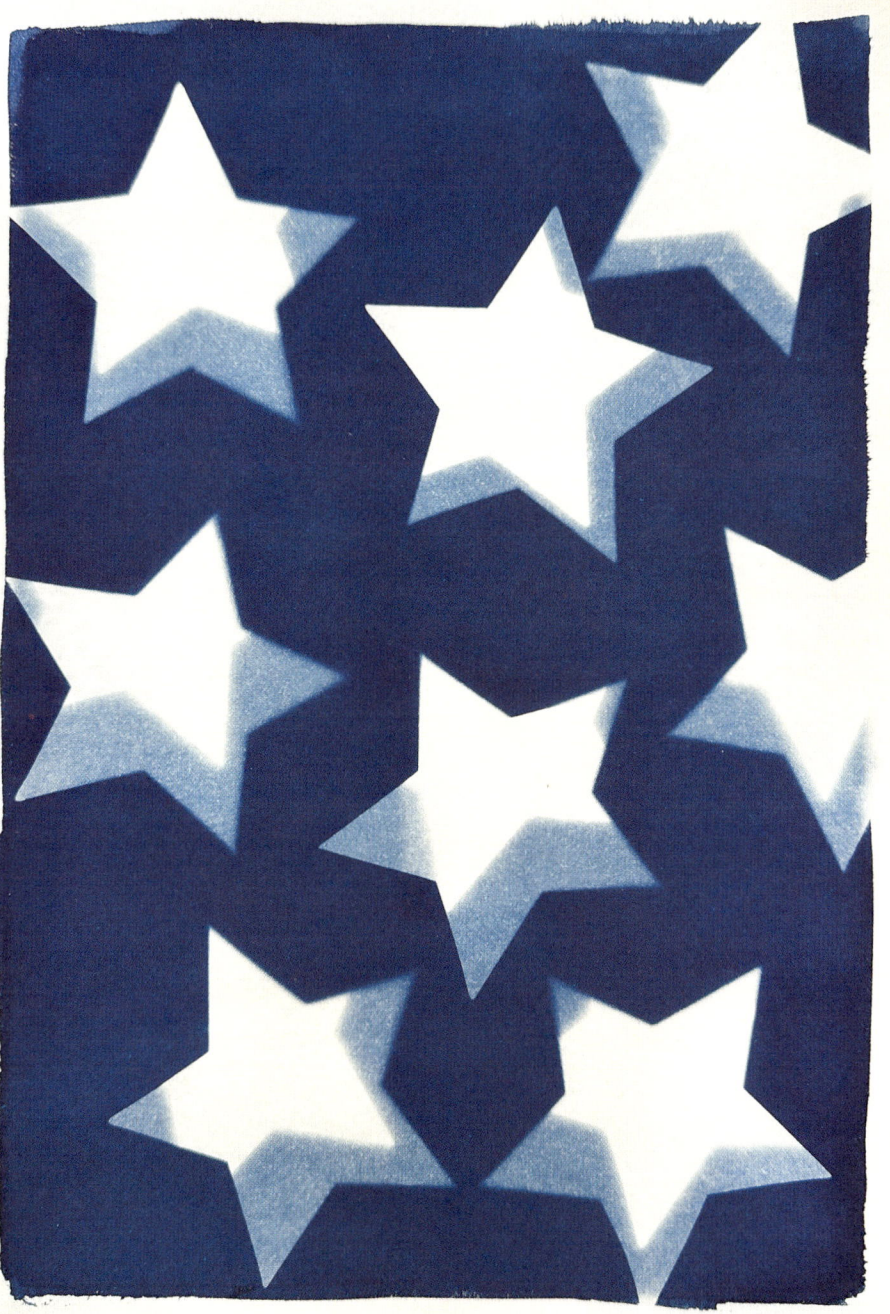

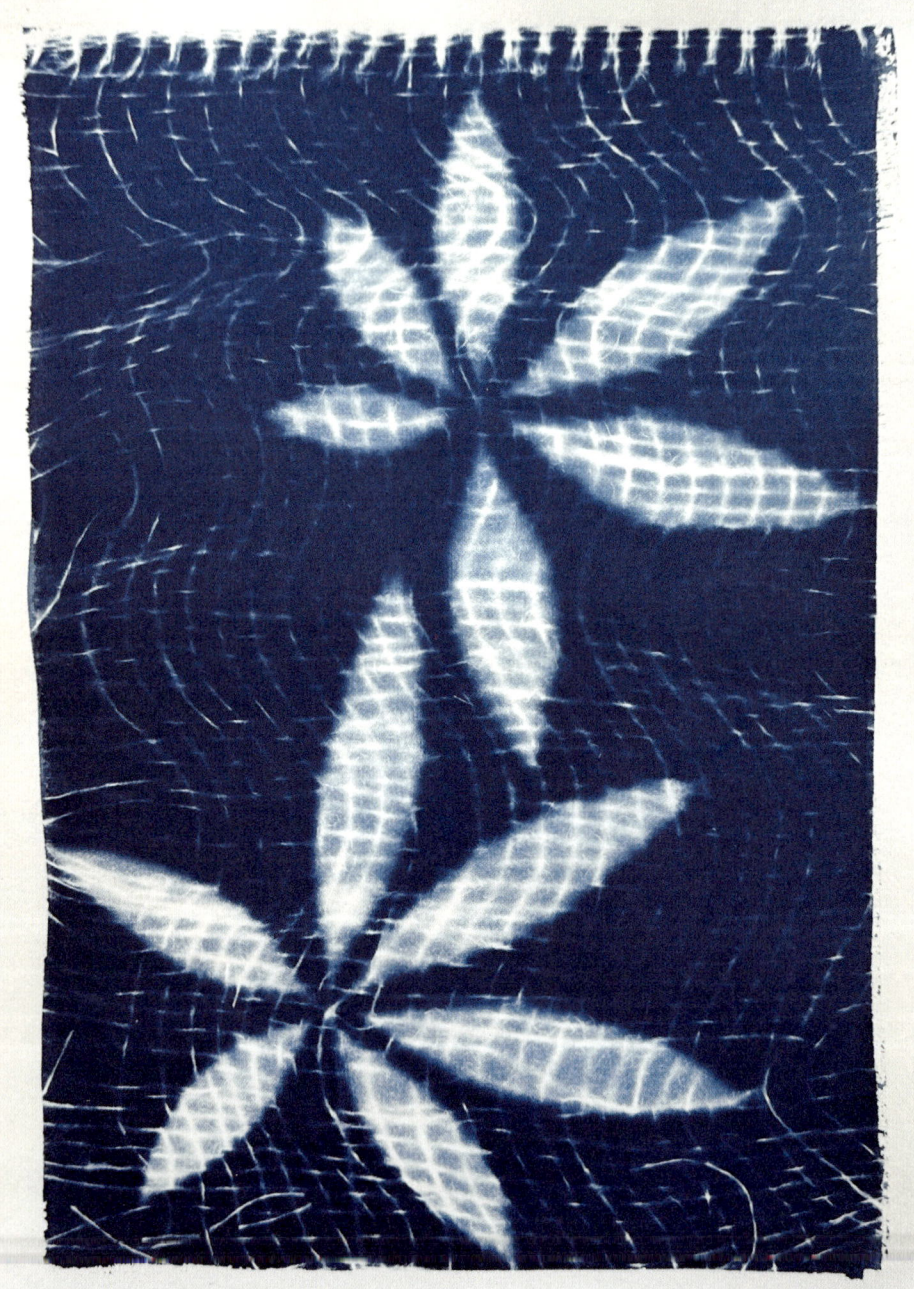

# Layering with textures

Another technique you could try is to leave the texture layer on the print after the initial exposure, adding your objects on top of the texture for the second exposure. The idea is that if the texture layer is bold enough, it shouldn't overexpose too much and will remain when you add the objects on top for your second exposure.

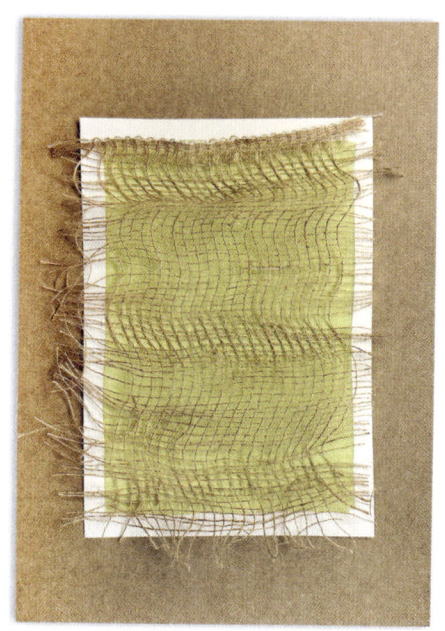

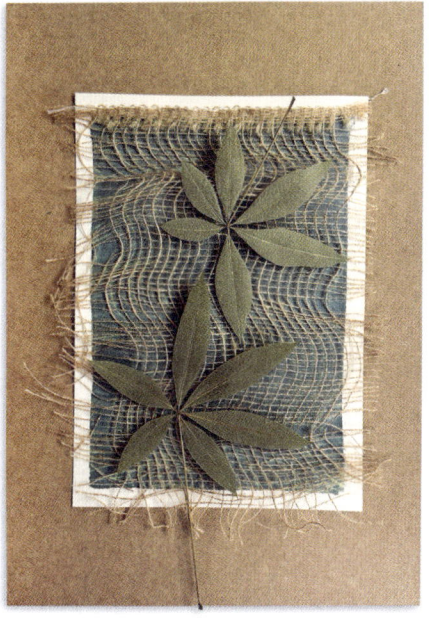

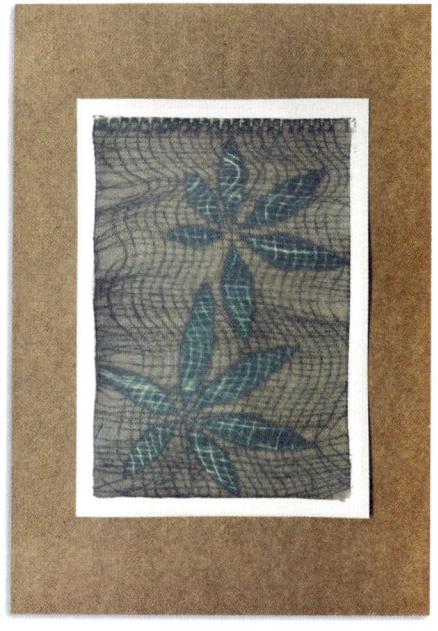

# Creative use of overexposure

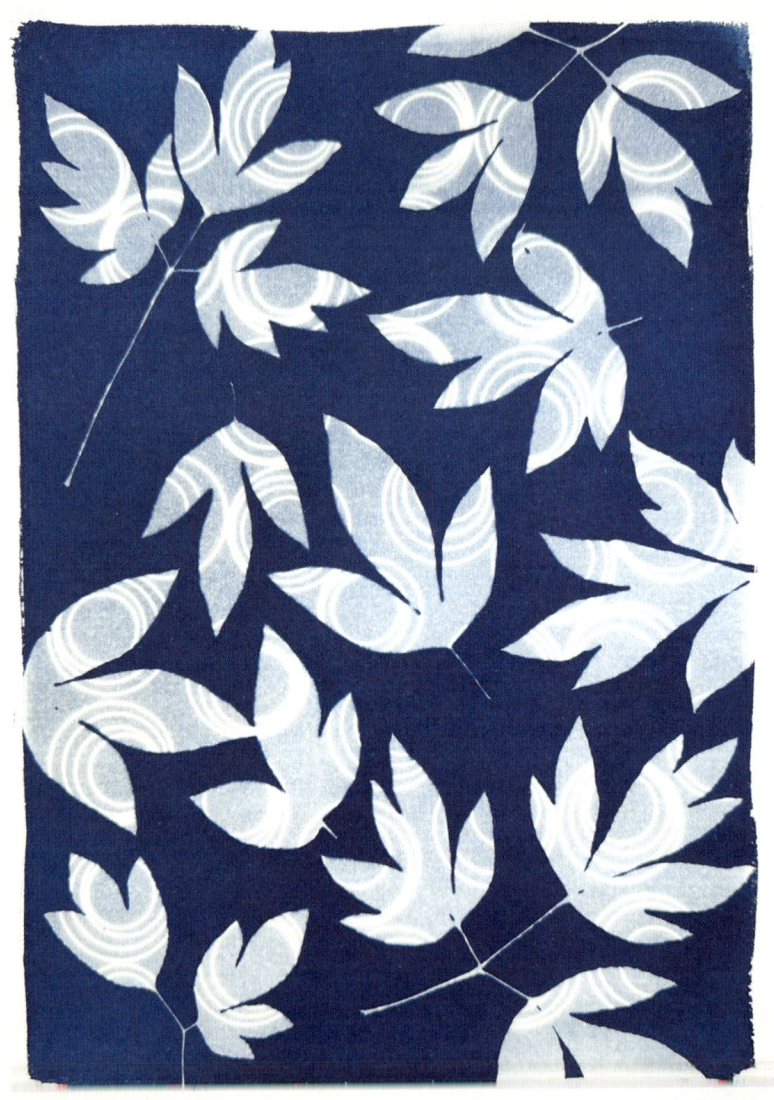

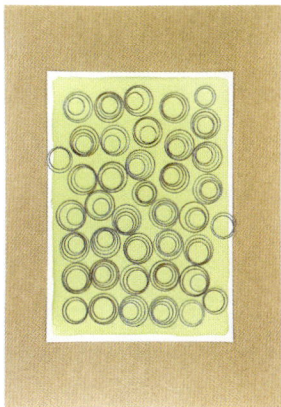

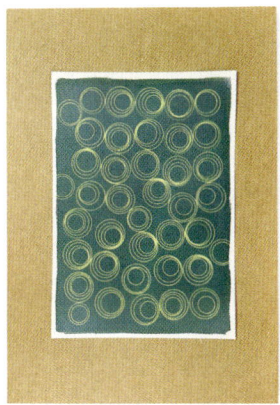

**1.** Choose your texture or create a pattern using objects for your first exposure. Expose for a short time – my exposure here was 15 seconds under a UV lamp but your own exposure will depend on the strength of the UV light source you are using (sun or UV lamp).

**2.** Remove your print from the light and remove all the objects you have just used to create your texture layer. For the second layer I tend to use bolder shapes like large leaves as I want the texture layer to be clearly visible inside the leaf shape. Lay the leaves down on your print over the already exposed area.

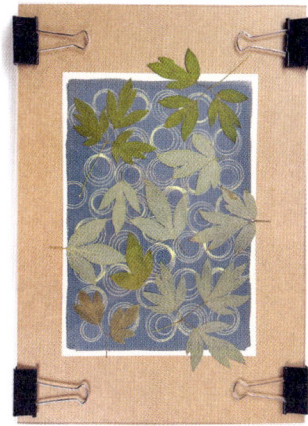

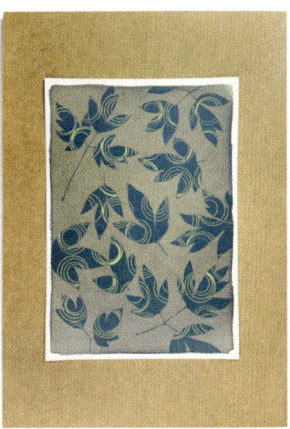

**3.** Expose your print for longer for this second exposure. I used a four-minute exposure under my strong UV lamp. If you are working outside, you might need to do a few test prints to get the results you are looking for.

**4.** Remove your objects, rinse well and dry. You will see that your first texture layer has overexposed and disappeared from everywhere apart from within your bold leaf shapes.

# Creating compositions using paper

**You don't have to rely on found objects or botanicals to create your cyanotype prints. You can cut out or tear shapes from paper or card to block the UV light. You can also use different weights and transparencies of paper, from tracing and tissue paper to thicker paper and card to layer up your composition.**

Start with just one exposure while you experiment with this technique. The steps on the opposite page show the effects of using three separate exposures to layer up your design to achieve different shades of blue. It helps to start by planning your composition.

**Below, left:** The shapes were cut from a sheet of paper, which was placed over the coated paper, leaving the leaf-shaped spaces blue.

**Below right:** The shapes cut from the paper on the left were used to create a new composition with multiple exposures.

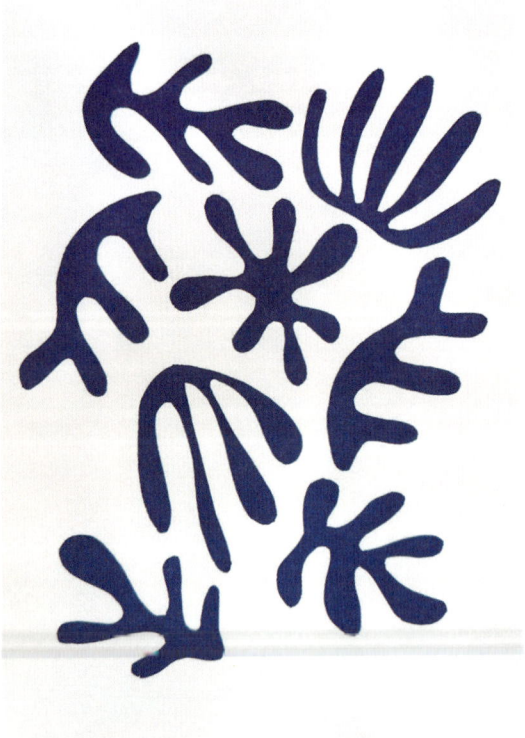
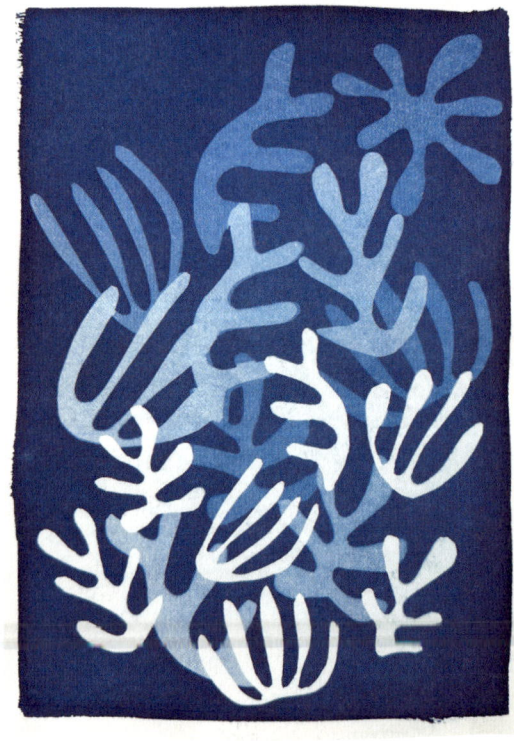

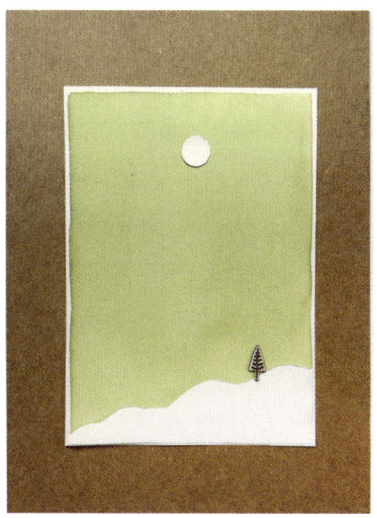

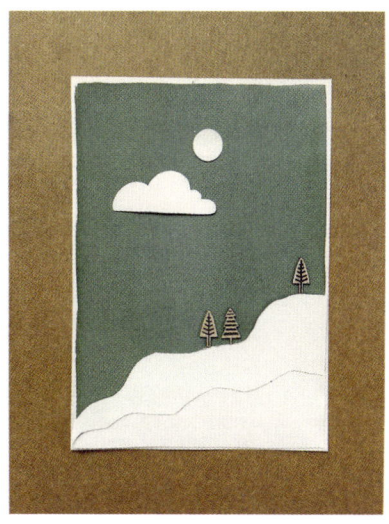

**1.** When you have decided on a design, plan which will be your white layer. This is the area of the print that will receive no light so whatever you place down first will remain white. Once you have this layer in place, cover it with Perspex and expose for a short while. My exposure was 15 seconds under a UV lamp but yours will take longer if using the sun.

**2**. Bring your print inside or remove it from under the UV lamp and add the second layer. Take care not to move the elements from your first layer. This second layer will be a pale blue. Expose your print for a short time again.

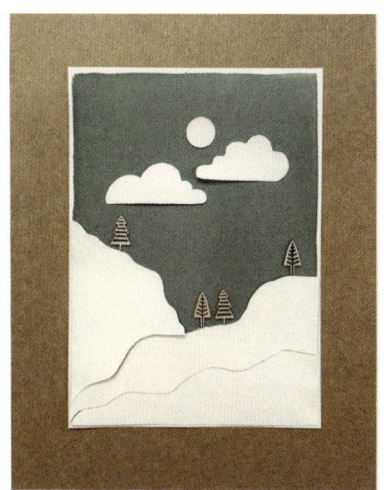

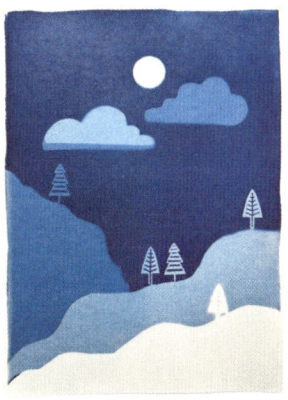

**3.** Now add the final layer. Again, take care not to move your first two layers (you can see in my final print that I accidentally moved the left cloud, but I like the 'shadowed' result all the same). This is going to be your last exposure so this time expose for longer to really develop the darker shades of blue.

# Projects

The previous chapters have shown you how adaptable and playful the cyanotype process is. Now you have the skills to create unique pieces for your home using fabrics and wood.

# Wooden decorations

Simple wooden decorations make great gifts – or just a beautiful statement for your own décor. Laser-cut plywood shapes of all kinds are available online and from craft shops and printing on wood is the same as printing on fabric or paper. You can make a string of individually printed and unique hearts for a loved one, or craft a festive display with beautiful, hand-printed stars strung across your mantlepiece.

## What you will need

- Cyanotype equipment, see pages 10–13
- Plywood shapes
- Ribbon or string for hanging

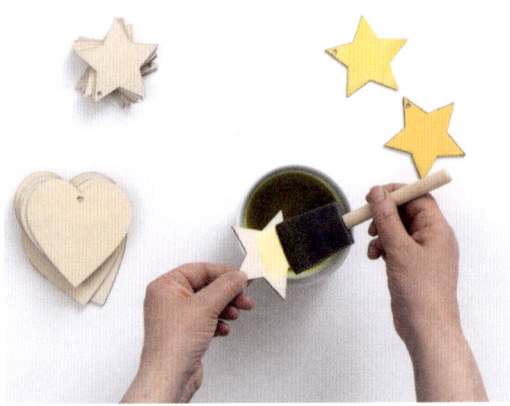

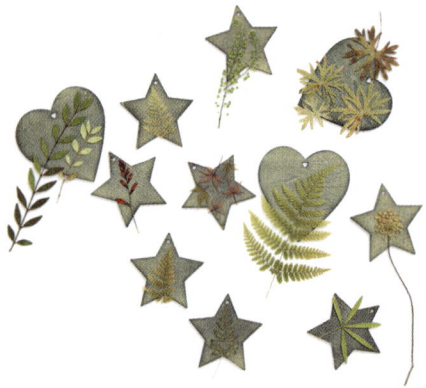

**1.** Coat the wooden shapes with the cyanotype emulsion and leave to dry in the dark. Think about whether you want to expose both sides of the shape or just one. If you are coating both sides, allow the side you coat first to dry before turning it over to coat the other side.

**2.** Lay out your wood shapes on your board and place your subjects on top. You could use botanical objects or lace, for example. Place your Perspex or glass on top of the shapes to secure and flatten your subject matter.

**3.** Expose your shapes in sunlight or UV light. You might find that exposures on wood take longer than exposures on paper or fabric.

**4.** Once exposed, remove your subject matter and rinse the wood shapes well in running water. Pat dry with paper towels.

**5.** String your pieces together or hang individually to make cyanotype decorations.

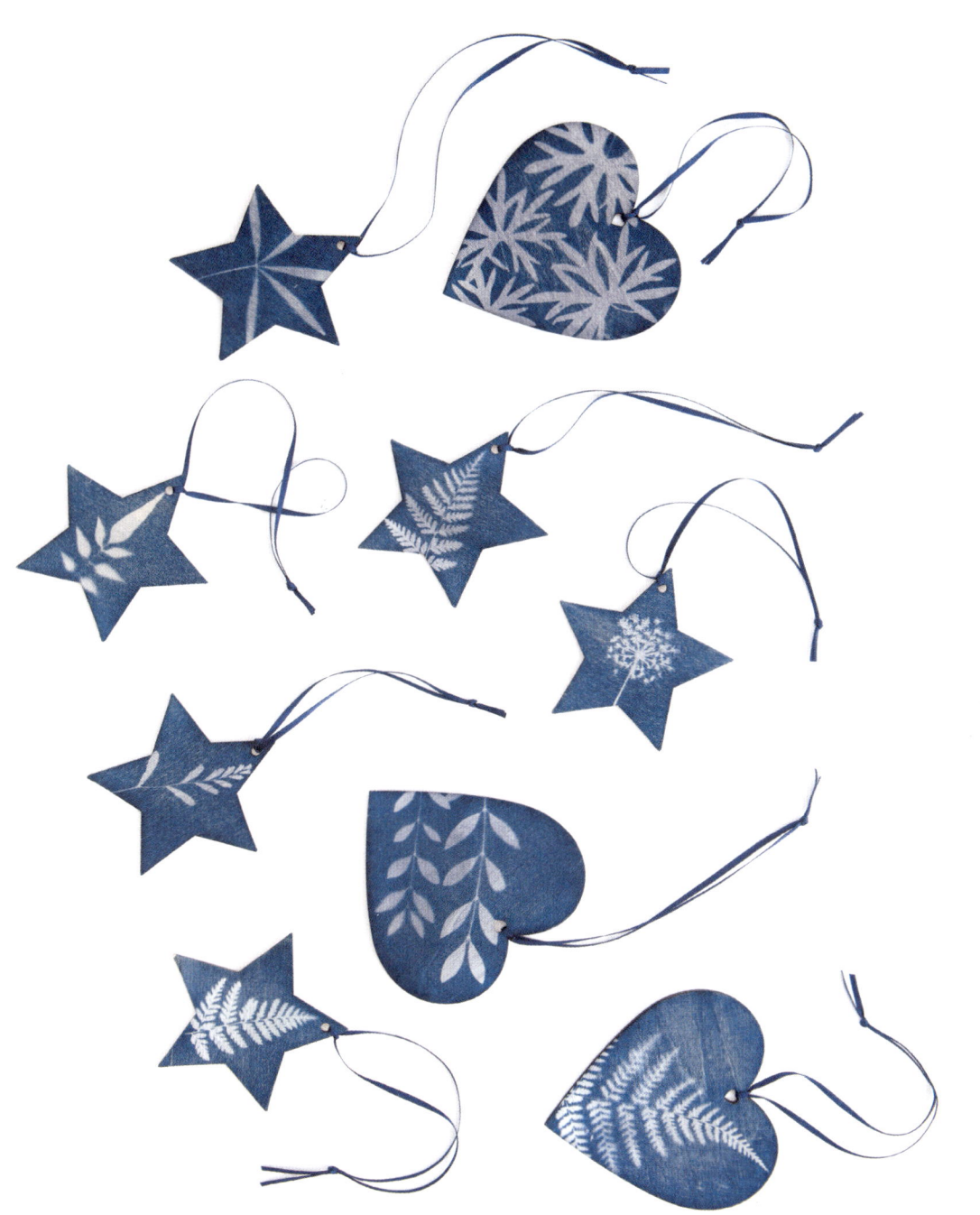

# Tote bag

Tote bags are a fun way of taking your unique cyanotype artworks off the wall and out into the world.

## What you will need

- Cyanotype equipment, see pages 10–13
- Plain white tote bag
- Cardboard
- Plastic wrap
- Masking tape
- Lace doilies for printing (or other objects)

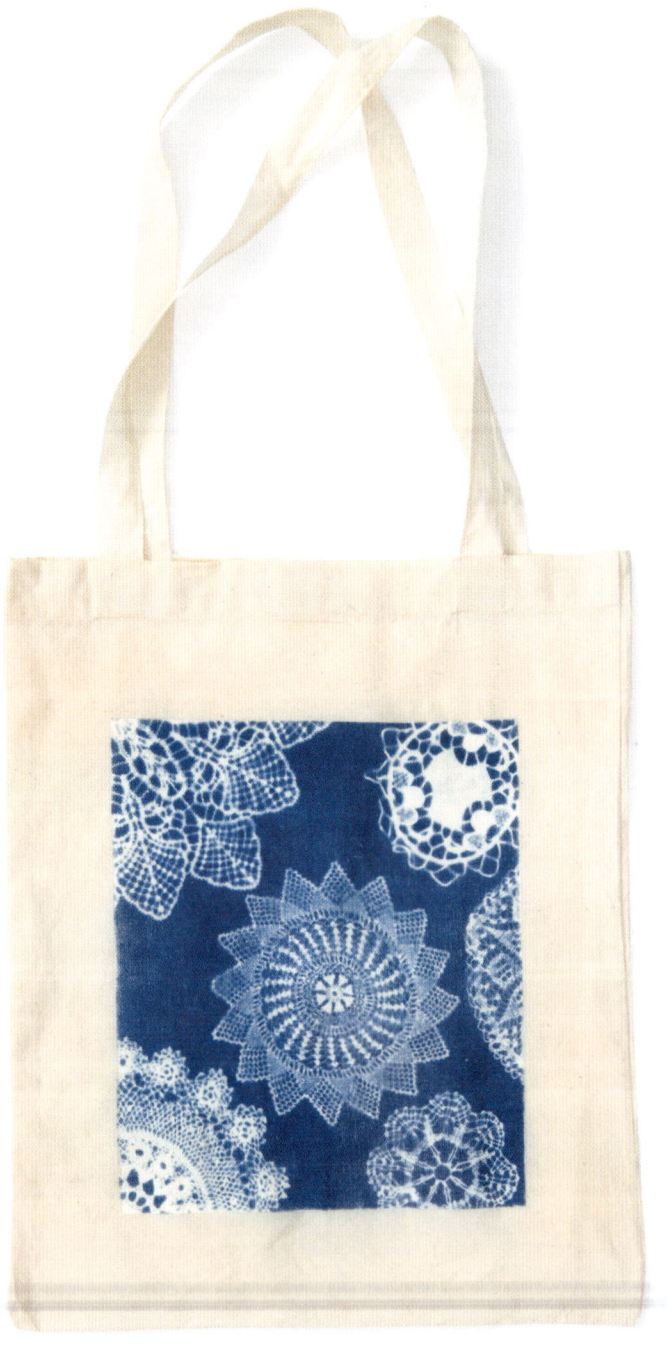

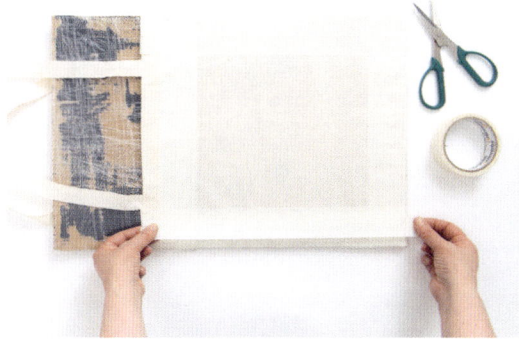

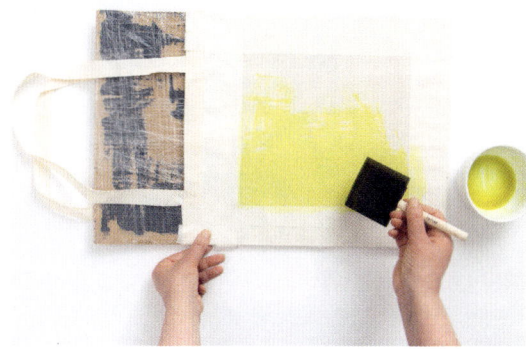

**1.** Place a piece of cardboard inside the bag to stop the chemicals bleeding through to the back of the bag. I wrap my cardboard in plastic wrap so that I can wipe it down afterwards and re-use it. Use masking tape to mask off the area you would like to print, if you want a tidy rectangle.

**2.** Paint the front of the bag with the cyanotype emulsion. Then leave to dry in a dark place such as a box, drawer or cupboard (remember to protect surfaces from staining).

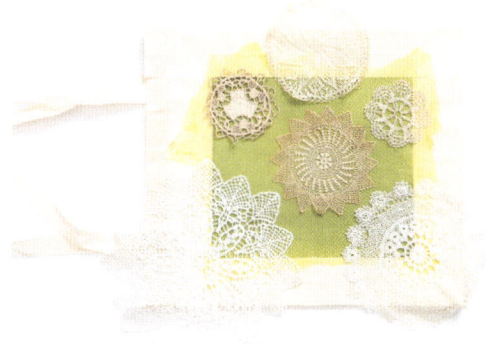

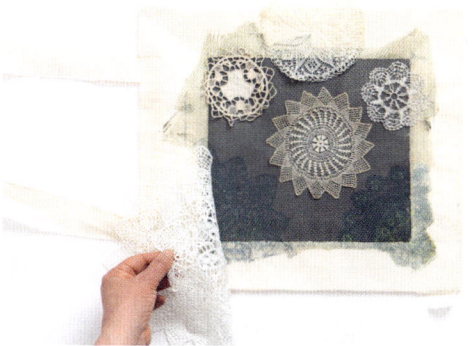

**3.** Plan out your design before exposure. Use a piece of Perspex or glass (making sure it is larger than the area you have coated) to flatten your objects down. Take outside or place under a UV lamp and expose. If you are exposing your bag outside, I recommend a quick test print beforehand to gauge the UV levels (see page 15).

**4.** Remove the objects you've used and rinse the tote bag thoroughly in water until the water runs clear. If you don't rinse out all of the chemicals, they will continue to expose slightly and you won't have clear whites in your finished print. Peg it up to dry and then iron it.

# Lampshade

Using cyanotype to make a lampshade is especially appropriate as it re-illuminates your light-powered artwork. Kits for lampshades are available from art and craft shops or online. They come in various sizes and consist of a sticky PVC-backed panel, two metal rings and strong double-sided tape. The kit used here is for a 25cm (10in) drum. The size of your lampshade will be dictated by the size of Perspex or glass that you use to press down your objects.

## What you will need

- Cyanotype equipment, see pages 10–13

- Fabric – enough to cover the PVC panel in the lampshade kit

- Objects for printing

- Iron

- Lampshade kit

- Scissors or rotary cutter and cutting mat

## Fabric

Choose natural fibres such as cotton or linen. Linen has a lovely texture when lit up, while cotton gives a crisp and smooth finish because the weave of the fabric is tighter than linen.

## Lampshade kit

Remember that you will need to dry your fabric in the dark, so take that into consideration when deciding on the size of your lampshade: the larger the lampshade, the longer the piece of fabric you will be coating and working on.

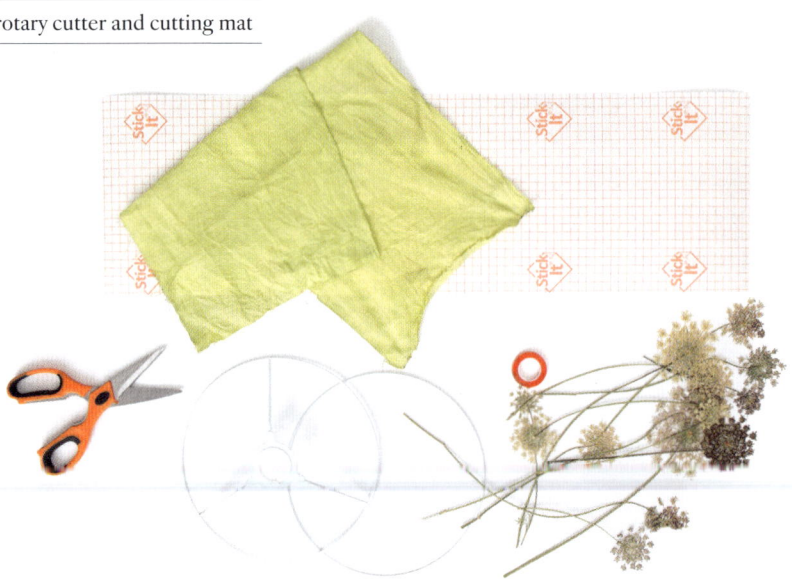

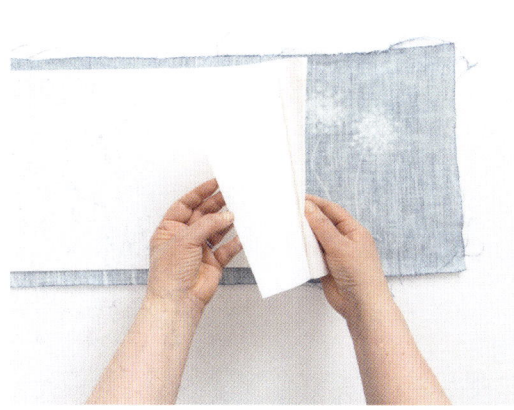

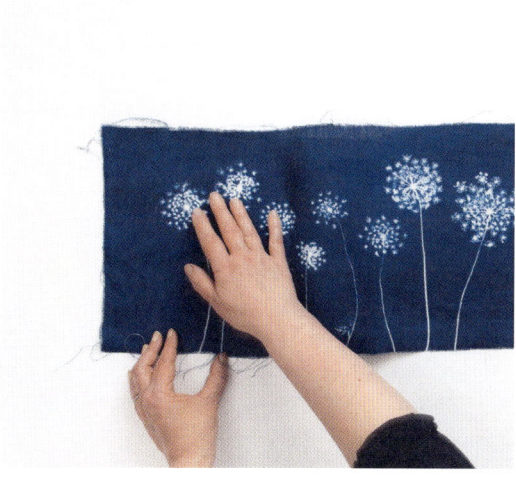

**3.** Once your fabric is dry, iron it well and lay it out flat before sticking on the PVC panel. Working slowly, peel away the backing paper and smooth down the fabric as you go, gradually working along the length of the panel.

**4.** To avoid wrinkles, it helps to keep turning the fabric and backing panel over as you work so you can check the fabric is smoothly attaching to the panel.

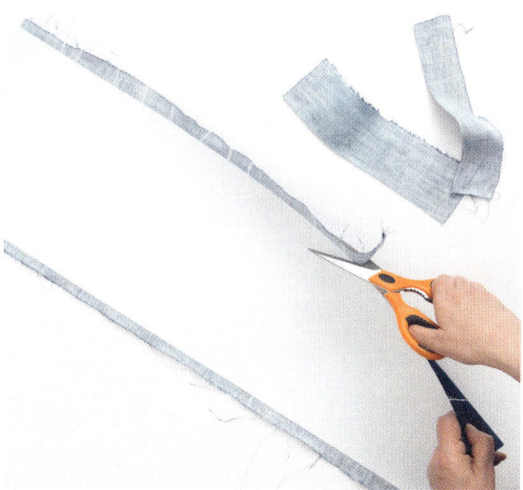

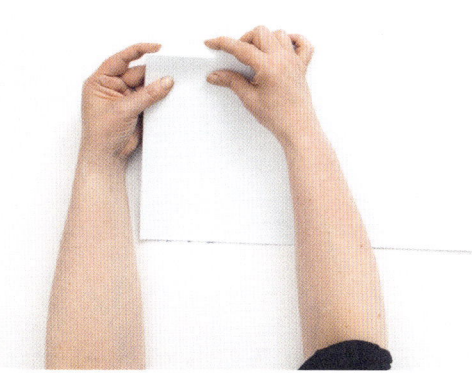

**5.** Trim away the excess fabric from the edges. Use scissors or a rotary cutter and cutting mat if you have one. Stay as flush to the edges as you can.

**6.** The PVC panel will have kiss-cut strips along on the top and bottom edges. Fold them back and crease along the cut lines, which will allow you to peel away the strips, leaving a fabric margin that you will later tuck under the rings. Work slowly and gently to avoid too much fraying. of your fabric. Snip away any loose threads.

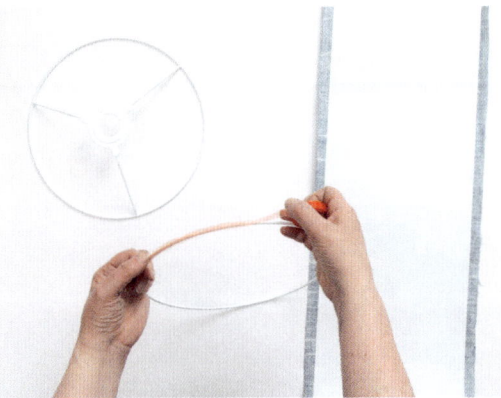

**7.** Attach a strip of double-sided tape along one side edge of the PVC panel: this will overlap with the other side edge when you construct your lampshade. Peel away the backing. Your panel is now ready to attach to the rings.

**8.** Attach the double-sided tape to both rings by running the tape all the way round the outside of each ring, pushing the tape down and around the ring with your finger and thumb so that it covers as much of the ring as possible. Decide the orientation of your shade – is it a pendant shade or a lamp base shade? That will decide where you place the ring with the spokes. A lamp base shade will have the ring with the spokes at the bottom of your design. Peel away the backing from the tape when you are ready to roll the shade.

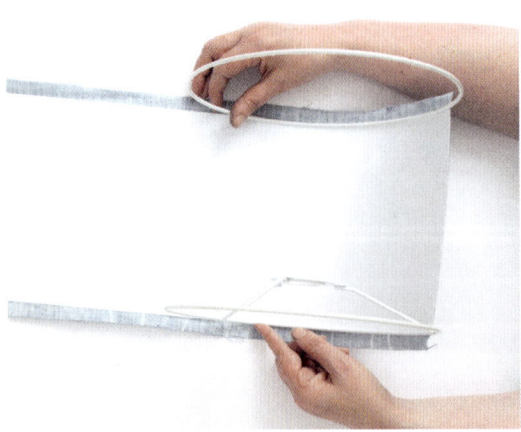

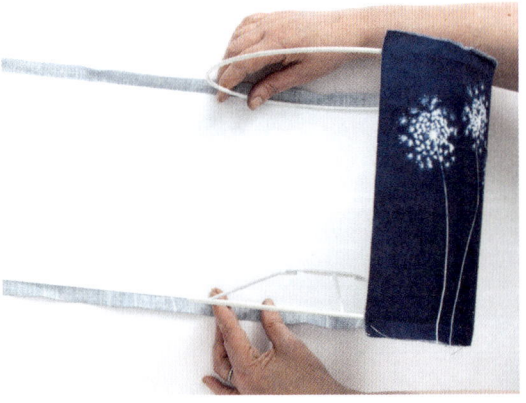

**9.** Place your rings on the top and bottom edges of the PVC panel, making sure that the ring with the spokes is facing into the centre, at the side edge without the sticky tape. Slowly roll both rings together along the PVC panel so it sticks to the rings as you go.

**10.** Keep rolling until the two side edges join together and are secured by the strip of sticky tape that you attached in step 6. Place the lampshade seam-side-down on the table and press down a few times to make sure that the seam is properly secured.

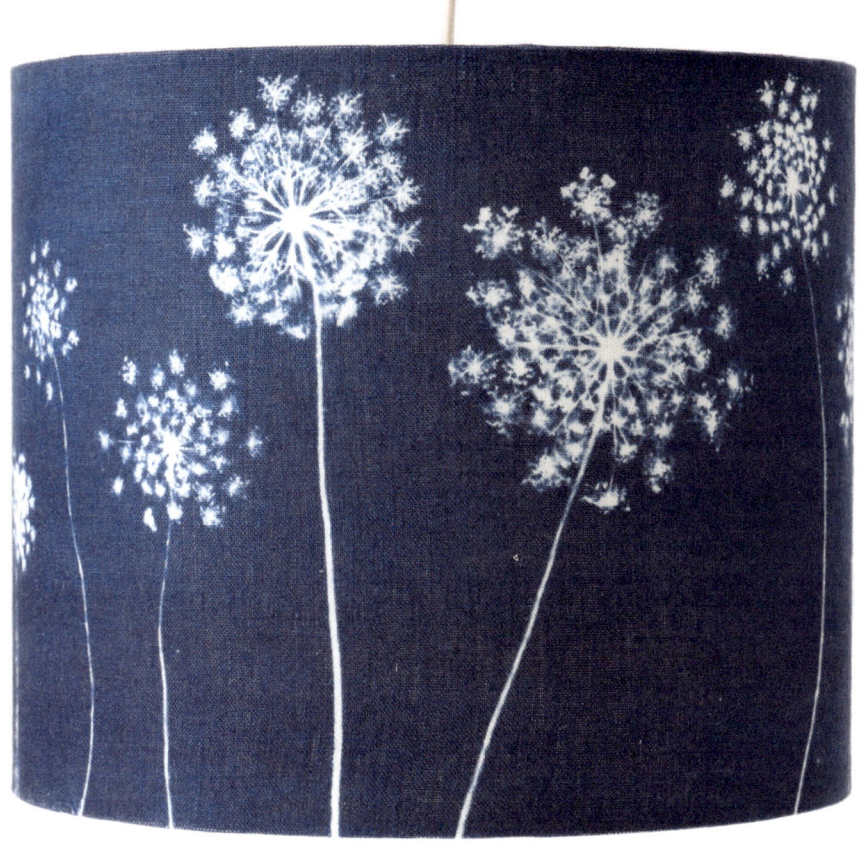

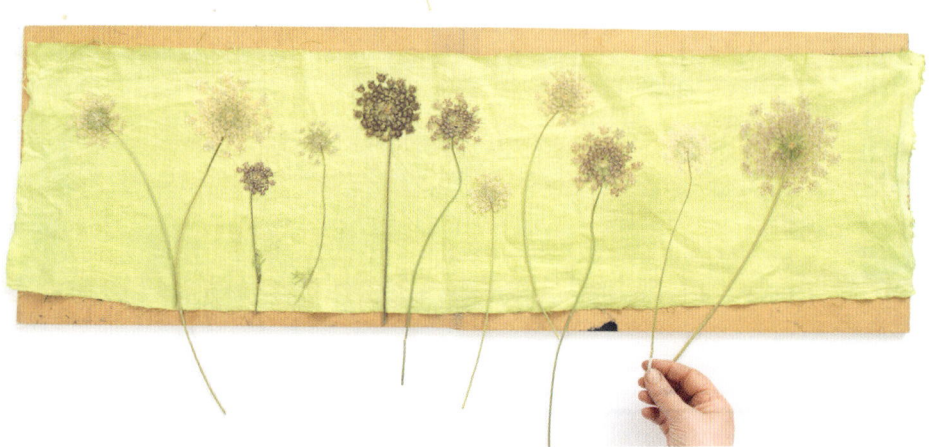

**1.** Coat the fabric with emulsion and then dry it. Hanging it up will help it to dry evenly but you can also lay it out flat. It may pick up some textures where it touches the surface it dries on – all these variables add to the interest and beauty of cyanotype prints. Take care to protect your surfaces from the fabric dripping or splashing.

**2.** Lay out the dry fabric on a board and arrange your objects. If you are using sunlight, you will need to carry the fabric with your design outside, so use a large and sturdy board to steady everything. Place (or clamp) your Perspex or glass sheet on top of the fabric and expose. Remove the objects and rinse the fabric well until the water runs clear.

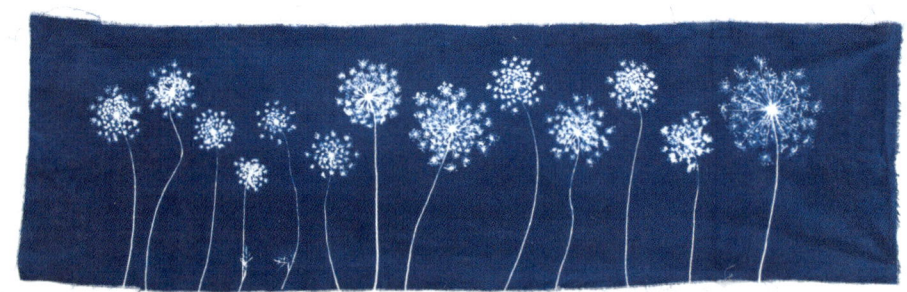

### Final composition

Bear in mind you will be trimming about 2cm (¾in) from the top, bottom and sides. Think about where your left and right sides will join once wrapped around the rings. You don't want the design to be cut off or to overlap, but you don't want too much of a gap either.

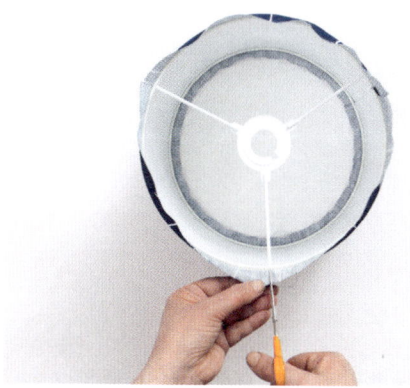

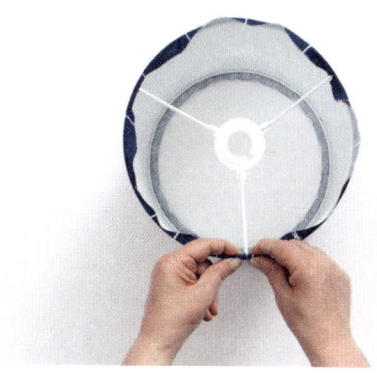

**11.** Carefully snip the fabric at each spoke so that you will be able to fold the fabric down neatly on either side of the spoke.

**12.** Push the fabric down so that it adheres to the glue on the rings. Do this top and bottom, taking your time to avoid creases.

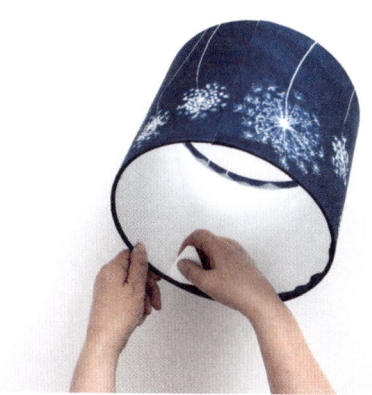

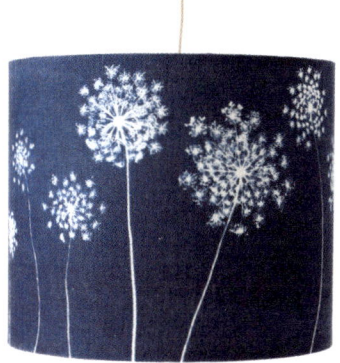

**13.** The final step is tucking the fabric under the rings. If you are using a lampshade kit, there should be a little plastic tool to assist with this, but otherwise you could use the corner of a bank card. This can be a fiddly step, especially around the spokes, but take your time and all of the fabric will tuck away neatly.

**14.** Attach your chosen light fitting and bulb and enjoy your beautiful creation.

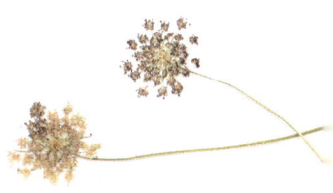

## Suppliers

**Cyanotype chemicals**
Jaquard: jacquardproducts.com

**Lampshade-making supplies**
Dannells: dannells.com

**Paper**
Fred Aldous: fredaldous.co.uk

**Fabric**
Whaleys Fabrics: whaleys-bradford.ltd.uk

## About the author

Victoria Glover is a printmaker and designer based at The Cyan Studio in Manchester where she runs workshops specializing in the cyanotype process. Trained at degree level in both photography and surface pattern design, the two disciplines have helped to shape her unique approach to cyanotypes.

Follow on Instagram: @the_cyan_studio

## Acknowledgements

A massive thank you to my husband Tom and my parents, Val and Con, for all being so supportive over the years. I wouldn't be doing any of this without your help. Thank you also to Zara for this incredible opportunity and for having faith in me. I've loved seeing your vision come to life. Thank you to Charles for the fantastic photos, too.